the naked coach

658
467
'24

bus~~iness coaching~~
~~made simple~~

david taylor

First published 2007 by
Capstone Publishing Ltd. (a Wiley Company)
The Atrium, Southern Gate, Chichester, PO19 8SQ, UK.
www.wileyeurope.com
Email (for orders and customer service enquires): cs-books@wiley.co.uk

Other Wiley Editorial Offices
John Wiley & Sons Inc., 111 River Street, Hoboken, NJ 07030, USA
Jossey-Bass, 989 Market Street, San Francisco, CA 94103–1741, USA
Wiley-VCH Verlag GmbH, Boschstr. 12, D-69469 Weinheim, Germany
John Wiley & Sons Australia Ltd, 42 McDougall Street, Milton, Queensland 4064, Australia
John Wiley & Sons (Asia) Pte Ltd, 2 Clementi Loop #02–01, Jin Xing Distripark, Singapore 129809
John Wiley & Sons Canada Ltd, 22 Worcester Road, Etobicoke, Ontario, Canada M9W 1L1
Wiley also publishes its books in a variety of electronic formats. Some content that appears in print may not be available in electronic books.

Library of Congress Cataloging-in-Publication Data is available on request

ISBN   978-184112-756-9

Anniversary Logo Design: Richard J. Pacifico

Set in ITC Garamond by Sparks (www.sparks.co.uk)
Printed and bound in Great Britain by TJ International Ltd, Padstow, Cornwall

This book is printed on acid-free paper responsibly manufactured from sustainable forestry in which at least two trees are planted for each one used for paper production. Substantial discounts on bulk quantities of Capstone Books are available to corporations, professional associations and other organizations. For details telephone John Wiley & Sons on (+44) 1243–770441, fax (+44) 1243 770571 or email corporatedevelopment@wiley.co.uk

This one's for you, for your teams and for your organization
That's the '**Who**'
The '**Where**' is wherever you are right now, whatever your experience and whatever your background
The '**What**' is business coaching, and this is not a book that spends 100 pages defining it – business coaching is quite simply:
Any and every intervention that enables
people, teams and organizations to be their very best
The '**When**' is now – right now, check the time as you read this – that's when this book is set
As for the '**Why**', it's exceedingly simple – because you can, and because, for those whose lives you touch, for your teams and organization, and for yourself, you must
Which leaves us only with the '**How**' ...
And to misquote Hamlet –
'**Herein, lies the rub ...**'
Inspired by *Inside Man*, screenplay by Russell Gewirtz

Roy McAvoy:
> 'This is everything, ain't it, this is the choice it
> comes down to, this is our immortality.'
His Caddy:
> 'You don't need to be thinking immortality,
> you need to think: "Hit the seven iron."'

From the film, *Tin Cup*

(Dis) Claimer
This is a work of fact. Any similarities to actual persons,
in real organizations, is entirely and deliberately intentional.

THE JOURNEY OF ...

PREPARE ...

This is your book, not mine. Read it as you choose, think whatever you think, write all over it and, above all, please do something as a result of what you read.

I have suggested six 'journeys'. However, the way I have structured this book does not matter. What matters is that you are spending your time and energy in reading it – make that time and investment pay by taking action to help yourself, those whose lives you touch, your team, a project at your organization.

This is your own, personal action journal.

That's 'action' journal. Not 'thought,' not 'debate' not 'discussion' journal.

This book is not written to be thought-provoking – it is written to be action-provoking.

And to help make that happen, it contains over 250 specific actions that you can take – the best of the very best.

If you heat a piece of metal in London, it will expand. If you then take that same piece to Cairo, Moscow, New York, and Auckland, it will also expand. It will always 'work'.

And so will the actions in this book. Do not misunderstand me; I am not an academic, I am not a guru, I am just an ordinary guy who has had the great fortune to work with hundreds of organizations and thousands of leaders, and experienced what works, what does not – when, why and how.

The Naked Coach is not an HR or leadership idea. It is a living, breathing set of actions, behaviours and choices that together will lead to the transformations that you have been looking for, and spending time and money on, for many years.

So it is time, now, to move from a 'can-do' attitude, to an 'am-doing' reality – in performance, perception and customer service – leading to repeatable and sustainable financial benefits.

The Naked Coach covers all of your life. This is because ... well, have you ever noticed, that wherever you go, there you are?

And because people (you) are not the number one asset in your organization – people (you) are the *only* asset in your organization. Indeed – you are your organization.

The fundamental of Naked Coaching is to be yourself – always. Success does not lie in taking less work home; it lies in bringing more of yourself to work – more of your personality, your ideas and your passion.

So, what works for you, all of you, works for you, all of you.

Please – enjoy reading, and make all of your dreams come true.

And if it is a choice between those two – please go for the latter, every time.

■

If you know the combination to the lock,
it doesn't matter who you are;
It has to open for you.

Orrin C. Hudson

■

And open for you it will.

With my very best wishes,

David

Journey One

Coaching from a Different Perspective – Yours

Journey One – Coaching from a Different Perspective – Yours

YOU, HERE, NOW

When you were young, you believed in yourself, you were confident and happy. Those feelings have not been lost, they have not disappeared; they are simply buried within you, and whether you unleash them *is your choice, and yours alone.*

Often, when I speak at conferences, I am introduced with the 'striptease' music. Every time I have to react as if it is the first time – like the Mars salesperson who hears the 'Look, it's the man from Mars' a dozen times a day.

They do this because they think I am the 'naked' leader, or coach.

And I am not.

They are.

You are.

Please be in no doubt, once and for always. Everything I write about is in the public domain. Everything I write about you already know, deep down. And everything I write about is obvious. All I have done is stripped away any jargon, mystery or hype.

Because, as I have said many times before, and will say many more times in this book, it is not only your birthright to be successful, by your own definition, it is your birthright to know how to be successful, at any time, and anywhere.

I read the books that you haven't the time to, I gather the material so that you don't have to. All I do is present it in a very simple way.

Which I have to, as it is the only way I understand.

The Naked Coach is about you:

All of you – the you at home, the you at work, the you that leads you, and the you that follows you around. The you that already knows, deep down, what you want and need to do in your life, in your teams, in your organization.

And what's more, I don't even mind if you believe me on this one. In fact, I would prefer if you don't believe in me at all. I want to know if you believe in you.

So, my first question: if not you, then who?

■

If not you, then who?

■

Are you in ownership of your life?

Simple test to see if you are in ownership of your life – to do right now. Think about someone in your family, or in your team at work. Someone whom you talk about a lot, when they are not there. Next time you are with them, perhaps just the two of you, tell them what you think, to their face. Be pleasant, be respectful, be professional. However, it is time to stop speaking *about* that person, and speak *to* that person.

■

This is a key moment in your journey of self-coaching – you can either do something about it, or simply read on. All you have to ask yourself, indeed the ultimate question of self-coaching, is –

■

Does what I am thinking/feeling/doing serve me or others, or not?

■

If you are not in ownership of your life, who is?

We all want to be popular, well liked. However, do you take it one stage too far – do you need it? If you do, if other people or outside events dictate how you feel about yourself, you are not in ownership. Someone else is.

You must be in ownership of your life, if you are going to coach yourself.

You must be in ownership of your life, if you are going to coach others.

And, most fundamentally, you must be in ownership of your life, if you are going to make your future, your choice.

■

What do you think? Your Future – By Chance or … Your Future – Your Choice?

■

Decide which you believe, right now. If you decided 'Chance', read on. If you decided 'Choice', do not read the next paragraph; go to the one beginning with '*Choice*'.

■

Chance

Congratulations – you are absolutely right, always have been and always will be. And each and every day, this thing we call 'life' will conspire to support your belief – if you believe that such moments are out of your control and only come along now and then, that is what will happen, because it will become self-fulfilling.

■

OK, so you read that paragraph, anyway.

■

Choice

Congratulations – you are absolutely right, always have been and always will be. And each and every day, this thing we call 'life' will conspire to support your belief – if you believe that such moments are within your control and come along when-ever you choose, that is what will happen, because it will be-come self-fulfilling.

■

So, if you believe you need to wait for such moments to come along, then wait. When and if they do, please rejoin the book then. And, if you believe the second, what you read and what you do next will have a transformational impact on your life.

I love those words 'a transformational impact'. 'Transformational' is something way beyond 'Change'. If you freeze water, it becomes ice. Yet, when melting it reverts to water. These are changes. Temporary shifts in state. If you burn a stick of wood, it becomes ashes. It can never become wood again. This is transformation. When a caterpillar – a slow, creeping, wormlike creature – undergoes metamorphosis, it emerges as a delicate and beautiful butterfly capable of flight. This is transformation. A permanent shift in state. And I suppose the biggest transformation of them all was the big bang, the transformation into the known universe.

I use transformation as a description of the result of what you do.

▪

Only you can make that choice.
Only you can make that transformation.
Your life – your choice.

▪

The power of this book is yours – it is you, decided by, and only by you. This book is not about what you read, rather what you do with what you read. I believe there is one reason above all others that many, many books do not inspire people to take action – because most fall into one fundamental trap: *they assume the power of any communication is with the communicator.* And it is not.

▪

The power, and effectiveness, of any and all communication is with the receiver – you – and the action that you take as a result.

▪

Please don't get me wrong. That decision and action may not be to travel to the moon. It may be simply to do nothing and relax, or to tell someone you love them, and mean it. Or to receive love provided by someone close to you.

▪

Love plays a massive part in preparing people for a leadership role. I've been helping my fiancée (Claire), who is about to take on a leadership role at work, to build upon her confidence. I could teach her all of the numerous techniques I've learned over the years. However, I found the most effective way was simply to show love and trust in her. Even when I thought she might stray off track, I let her; and I made sure that I was there if she fell.

Tony Knill

■

What is a 'huge' decision for some may be 'small' for others. It is *your* decision, *your* life, *your* adventure. So this is your book, not mine. Because being a Naked Coach is about being you – it is about coming home to be who you already are. It is about finding success, by finding yourself.

Being successful, by being you.

In a world that so wants us to be like everyone else – as thin as … , as successful as … , as …

Imagine that everything you have ever done, all that you have ever known, and each thought you have ever had, comes down to this very moment. As you read this. Because it does, and to every moment that you live.

How powerful is that?

And how powerful are you?

Transformation, by being yourself. How cool is that? Having a transformational impact – on your own life – by simply being yourself.

In your life I expect you have heard the following phrases:

'You are good'

'You are bad'

'You are a great … '

'You are not so good at … '

And so the list goes on.

The words and opinions you heard and took on board as truths from the day you were born right up to this very moment as you read this.

I now offer you a different perspective:

You are

You are here, and now:

Wherever you have come from

Whoever you have met

Whatever you have done

And in that is a miracle so powerful and a truth so deep, that whatever you are thinking right now, as you simply realize that you *are*, perhaps you are filled with joy, energy and hope.

Think about what made you: the timing, synchronicity (coincidence?), and delicate biological tuning – the whole process of making you – is perhaps the finest example of sub-conscious self-coaching ever. An ovum needed to be regularly released each month from your mother's ovary, a process that could only proceed if a complicated cascade of hormonal events took place without interference. This egg then needed to be able to move freely along an unblocked Fallopian tube where it could be fertilized by a sperm and then reach the womb. The sperm had to be healthy, mobile and numerous, although only one ultimately penetrated the egg and formed an embryo with it. Think about that leading sperm, full of a desire for life – do you think it ever thought to itself, 'I don't feel like doing this today' or 'I think I'll give up now'?

▪

The many processes that must occur at precisely the right moment for the creation of you, were, and are, astounding.

▪

And the miracle continues: the lining of the womb had to be receptive to this embryo so that it could embed itself within it and begin to produce the hormones necessary to maintain the pregnancy thereafter.

Any one of these sensitive and essential components of fertility could easily be upset by a number of unfavourable factors that would have resulted in you not being here, and who you are, today.

If what people say about you is important to you, as it is to many, your birth-day was a critical day for you. Everyone rejoiced. Everyone. They asked you your weight without adding the word 'diet'. They looked at you and made 'gaga' noises without fear of their own embarrassment. And they loved you without condition. *Without condition.* And you so loved in return.

Love conceived you, love made you in the warmth of your mummy, and you were loved on the day that you were born.

▪

'It comes like the waves in the ocean,' my mother told me. 'Powerful, strong and rhythmic. Unceasing. Wave after

wave.' She was right. In labour with my son, my first child, he and I are carried over crest and trough, and we let go, freeing ourselves to be swept into birth. I feel and see my body writhing, snakelike and sensual as the waves come, one following the other. My body responds, knowing what to do. I let go. 'You can't fight the waves. Just let them carry you.' I hold her words in my mind, and, for one long holy moment, surrender myself to the magic, as I have never done before.

Deirdre Pulgram Arthen

■

Just four weeks after conception, your heartbeat could be detected! Your teeth buds appeared at 45 days after conception! Nine weeks after conception, your fingerprints, footprints and palm creases could be seen by ultrasound! On the day that you were born, you were 'perfect', and you still are, and always will be. Why do so many of us try to change perfection? And, more importantly, why do we so rarely accept perfection in ourselves?

■

A little girl walked to and from school daily. Though the weather that morning was questionable and clouds were forming, she made her daily trek to the elementary school. As the afternoon progressed, the winds whipped up, along with thunder and lightning. The mother of the little girl felt concerned that her daughter would be frightened as she walked home from school and she herself feared that the electrical storm might harm her child.

Full of concern, the mother quickly got into her car and drove along the route to her child's school. As she did so, she saw her little girl walking along, but at each flash of lightning, the child would stop, look up and smile. Another and another were to follow quickly and with each, the little girl would look at the streak of light and smile. When the mother's car drove up beside the child, she lowered the window and called to her, 'What are you doing? Why do you keep stopping?' The child answered, 'I am trying to look pretty. God keeps taking my picture.'

Paul Dinsmore

■

If you think that being born with a disability makes you or someone else imperfect, that is only your point of view, or choice. Being born blind, or deaf, or whatever, does not make you imperfect, unless you decide that it does. Andrea Bocelli was born blind ('No moments in my life have gone by without being filled with passion for music.'), as was Fanny Crosby (she wrote more than 8000 songs). Dummy Hoy, born deaf, was an outstanding player in Major League Baseball in the US. If you are dyslexic, you have a far greater statistical chance of being a millionaire. And so the list goes on.

■

> It is for us to pray not for tasks equal to our powers,
> but for powers equal to our tasks,
> to go forward with a great desire forever beating at the
> door of our hearts
> as we travel toward our distant goal.
>
> *Helen Keller*
> *Deaf and blind author, activist, and lecturer*

■

Our only real disabilities are the disabling choices we make.

On those days when you are feeling a bit down, or you feel like not giving or being your best, think about that moment when you emerged into the world. Did your mother say to herself on the day that you were born, 'I don't feel like giving birth today, so I don't think I'll bother'?

Someone said to me at a conference, 'I am a born cynic.'

'Trust me,' I told him, 'you're not. If you were a born cynic, you would never have come out of your mother in the first place.'

'And,' I added, 'you have only decided that recently.'

Please, show me a cynical child.

■

As the birth of my first baby is nearly here (two months to go!), I wondered to myself what are the questions that might help him or her in life, so I decided to write this; maybe one day it will help my 'little nipper' …

Dear Little Nip,
In times of crisis, we empower, we have a go and we forget the word 'can't'. We seem to go beyond any boundaries or limitations we once thought we had.

Take time to wonder at the possibilities you might create for yourself every day.

At times we will think that we are 'right' and everyone else is 'wrong' and will go to great lengths to prove it. Friendships break down, families fall out and we even go to war to show that we are right and others are wrong ... but at what cost? Idealism and getting the 'right answer' can be a great motivator and drive us forward; it can also get in your way and stop you from achieving anything at all.

So my little baby – use these questions to help you as they have helped me to create the wonderful life and opportunity we are creating together:

Limits – what limits?!

Am I just trying to be 'right' or could I be creating new amazing possibilities for others and myself instead?

Am I making the most of 'now'?

We only have now!

Lots of love

Mum xx

Fleur Wilkinson – Re-Innovate Ltd
Fleur works with a number of organizations, helping them to create business benefits through coaching and innovation cultures.

■

And then we have the other extreme – how you will be remembered after you die.

Tell me, have you ever been to a funeral where someone said, 'He could have done much better in this area' or 'She was not good at that'? Or read in the local paper that a person who has just died was a 'pain in the community who will not be missed'?

Transformation, by being yourself

I once shared this idea at a conference and the delegates and I had a thirty-minute debate on whether it was possible, whether it was logical and whether it was the correct use of English to say that one could transform by being oneself. Surely the term 'to transform' means to become something else? Frankly, fascinating though the discussion may be, it is irrelevant.

■

You have little time on this earth – as it says in *The Shawshank Redemption* – it is time to get busy living, or get busy dying.

■

We have talked and debated, and read and re-read enough, thank you very much. It is now time for action – to actually go out and take that first step towards your dream, your outcome, your result. And when you do that, and you succeed, if you want to call that success, or transformation, or a pair of curtains, I really don't mind. And you don't need to, either.

We spend so much time talking action and not enough taking action. We chat and discuss and analyse what we should or should not do – we even have business events and round-table dinners to do this. And we all get together and put forward our points of view and experiences, and we hear others' points of view and experiences.

And then what? At worst, we make sure our point of view prevails – which is absolutely pointless as no-one else will do anything about it unless they have chosen to. At best we are inspired. To do what?

There is no point in being inspired unless we actually do something with it. Inspiration is an energy that is just waiting to be used – and if it isn't, then it will simply run out. Like one of those helium balloons; release it at maximum energy and off it goes, on its journey. Left in a house, it slowly deflates and gets lower each day until it lies crumpled on the floor. These discussions and events and training courses are pretty much like that.

Up until now you either agree with me, or you don't. If you agree, please put this book down now and go do something.

I will say that again. You either agree with me, or you don't. If you agree, please put this book down now and go do something. Mark the book where you are and rejoin me later.

OK – you are not yet convinced, or you have taken that first step. Either way, that little voice in your head has started chatting away – and that little voice is most likely telling you to stop, to be careful, not to take a risk, not to make a mistake … Indeed, it is filling your mind with more reasons for inaction or why not to take the second step. And because it is your inner voice, and people tend to like to agree with themselves (otherwise madness quickly ensues), this voice is now sounding like the voice of reason.

It is actually the Voice of Excuse. And it specializes in four main excuses above all others – and they are:

- If you do that you, could lose everything – protect what you have
- If success was this simple, everyone would be doing it – you need to be convinced
- You need more information, more data and knowledge before you agree to make your first move
- You do not know what you want to do, or where you want to be

Four reasons for inaction, from the Voice of Excuse …

Excuse One: If you do that you could lose everything – protect what you have

I call this the fifty word excuse – and it goes something like this:

At an entrepreneurial seminar, a fellow delegate said to the speaker after the event, 'I wish I could do what you do,' to which the speaker replied, 'Why don't you, then?' And then the words came out – one on top of the other:

'I'd love to and I couldn't because I have a well paid job and a lovely family and I'd lose my career and my family and our house and be divorced and I'd be alone and then I'd be on the street and then I'd be desperate and have nothing to live for.'

It's always around fifty words, depending on how 'low' the low point – I call it the 'I'd be' paragraph of destruction – fifteen seconds from dream to despair while standing on the same spot. What wonderful games the mind can play.

I was working at Allianz-Cornhill in Guildford, when one day I decided to resign and leave a well paid job, to pursue my dream of writing and spreading the word on leadership. I had no promise of work, and no guarantee of income. It was the bravest, most exciting and most stupid thing I have ever done, and if I had my time over, I would have found a different way of making my dream happen.

■

> A high-performing employee in our company was in a dilemma – part of him wanted to quit and ride a Harley across the American Midwest, the other part wanted to make a success of his new role – a very challenging one. We arranged for him to spend time with an external coach, and the coach worked with him over a few months to help him clarify his priorities in the new job, recognize what success looked like and contextualize the role in relation to his personal career development. He discovered for himself that he only wanted to 'quit' because in many ways that was the easier option. The result? A happy, at-ease employee who is once again performing to his potential and relishing the fresh challenges and opportunities that the role brings. Oh, and he will soon be taking an extended holiday to ride that bike ...
>
> *John Botia*
> *HR Director – Scottish & Newcastle UK*

■

The idea that to pursue your dream means giving up everything that is dear to you is nonsense.

And that is the very last thing I would recommend you do, because:

- Success does not necessarily mean leaving your present company – indeed, it may be to stay and grow and find fulfilment.
- Success does not necessarily mean anything to do with work or your career.
- Success is yours – it is yours to own and no-one else has any right to tell you that your success is wrong, providing that you do not hurt, or damage, someone else.

If you have a dream, you have the power to achieve that dream. I truly believe that, and I am the last person to recommend that you give up what you have to pursue what you want. There are so many other ways.

Excuse Two: If success was this simple, everyone would be doing it – you need to be convinced

Success is indeed very simple, for anything in your life. Indeed, there is a simple formula that guarantees it:

■

Know what you want to do, or where you want to be
Know where you are now
Know what you have to do, to get to where you want to go, or where you want to be
And
Do it!

■

Simple, but that doesn't make it easy.

Not easy, because we have 'learned' (by being told over and over and over) that success is tough, and achieving it requires this qualification or that experience. And yet, when you think about everything you have done in the last 24 hours that you would call 'success' (achieving the result that you hoped for), you will find you followed this formula to the letter. Whether it was motivating your team, closing a sale with a customer, eating lunch, or simply going to the loo, you followed it.

You always have, you always do, and you always will.

So, everyone is doing it – including you. All I am asking you to do is to apply what you already know, and what you already do, to some of the bigger things in your life. Simple, yet not easy.

Because then we might have to face up to the possibility that we can be more, that we can achieve our wildest dreams, that we can take that first step. And that makes us excited, and uncomfortable.

Fine, that is what this book is here to help you with, so get over excuse number two now – success is a formula, it is simple and it is available to you, right now.

Excuse Three: You need more information, more data and knowledge before you agree to make your first move

In which case put down this book now and go and lie down. You need it – you have learned so many facts about success, you have heard so many ideas about achieving your dreams, you have found so many people who are happy to give you their advice on turning your personal life into an adventure. And yet now, you feel you want some more.

OK – this book will provide you with specific ways to achieve success. I simply ask of you one thing – be aware of the skills, talent and knowledge that you already have.

Yes, this book is full of tips and actions and 'How-To's. However, I am no longer going to pander to your false belief that before you take that first step, you need more. You decide you are going to take that first step and I will help you take it.

Whatever you want in life, you have massive power and potential to make it happen, to bring it closer – and

■

there is no point having such huge potential, if you do nothing with it.

■

I had to find a breakthrough with a member of my team – I knew he was planning an extension to his home, and asked how this was going. He gave me a catalogue of reasons why this had not progressed. After he finished his long list there was silence. I let the silence happen, and it was he who broke it, to say there was 'no reason, really'. Perhaps two of the most powerful tools we have in business coaching – silence, and relating what we discuss to other areas of our lives. Both seem to work, every time.

Keith Newman

■

A question from a conference in Cape Town

'David, is what you have shared with us today, this idea that we have everything we need to be anything we want already within us, provable, in hard scientific, logical, analytical terms?'

I thought for a moment and then answered: 'No.'

Everyone at the conference reacted differently. What I said next came simply from my heart, and was something like this:

'Why do we always put so much importance on things having to be measured, or proved, or analysed? Why do we have to think through ideas and choices in our own heads before we go out and do something, or before we take ownership, or we awaken to the possibility we have incredible talent, just as we are. Surely, for whatever we think in life, we can always find so-called evidence that we are right or wrong? I am not sure any one course of action can be a catch-all solution or way forward for everyone, because we are all different, with different challenges and dreams, and on different journeys. I am sure – I am absolutely certain – that all of this thinking and avoiding decisions and action until we have proved what we are about to do will work, is one of the main excuses we use for not achieving our destinies, or from taking our organizations forward.

'What about how we feel about an idea, about a choice, about anything? Have we as a society become so embedded in the importance of knowledge that we have forgotten the power of our own instincts, our own hearts? We are so obsessed with the word, with the graph, with the statistic. I believe it is time to go with the heart, with the gut, with our feelings.'

And of course, as with anything, we can always quote sources that support what we say, in this case the brilliant *Blink* by Malcolm Gladwell.

And we rarely quote sources that disagree with what we say, in this case the brilliant *The Devil's Chaplain* by Richard Dawkins.

Read these if you choose – or next time you have a decision to make. Listen with your head, and go with your heart.

■

Excuse Four: You do not know what you want to do, or where you want to be

AHA!!! The BIG ONE.

When we release that potential, even if we think about the release of that potential, our heart leaps. And then we think about that new power we would have, and that world of uncertainty, and just as quickly, our heart sinks.

Exciting as 'Transformation' is, it also brings with it huge fear.

I was opening a two-day leadership event and started with the words 'Welcome to an experience that will have a transformational impact on you, on those whose lives you touch, on your communities, your teams and your organization, if you so choose'.

One person said that they had a 'problem' with that – and with anything that made such a big, positive claim. Indeed, hearing those words put him off the event, and made him decide that the event would have no such impact. I apologized, and said:

'OK. If it helps you more, welcome to an experience that will have no impact whatsoever on you, on those whose lives you touch, on your communities, your teams and your organization, if you so choose.'

Because, although so many of us are looking, waiting, hoping for that magic moment, that master key, that secret revealed, that will bring us what we seek – peace of mind, freedom, and ultimate happiness – we greatly fear the unknown.

And so we convince ourselves that transformation cannot be within our control, almost that we would rather be uncomfortable with what we know than move into the unknown. And to support this view, we look at other people – after all, if it was this simple, more people would be happy, and fulfilled, and the world would be a better place.

And so we conform – we become much like everyone else and keep our true self and dreams and ambitions to ourselves.

Until that very moment when we decide 'That's it, enough, I am now going to do something – for myself, for someone else, for my team, for my company, for my world. I am going to stand up and be counted'.

That moment is now, if you so choose.

To know that this really is one of those special, almost unique moments where we can take a big decision in our lives. When we feel in control, rather than being controlled. When you are ready for something big to happen. And as you read these words and think about that possibility, perhaps your heart is beating slightly louder with excitement, your body is buzzing with energy, and your whole being is ready, in anticipation.

All of our lives come down to such moments. And, by deciding that this is such a moment, we give ourselves a power to make a decision, to take an action, as opposed to simply waiting for such moments to come along (I find it fascinating that so many people, teams and organizations do such waiting).

For this book is your book, it is your life, and if you are brave enough, if you dare to make that decision, I promise you that you will not be alone. And more so, that you will never, ever regret it.

So, you are ready to take ownership of your life, to look at the choices before you on something that is important. And to make a decision.

How do you do that?

You simply do it – you make a decision on the 'What'.

And you make it in a moment, with a single blink of your eyes, in a heartbeat. Wherever you are, on a train, at home, wherever. Whenever you are, whatever age. And, whoever you are, woman or man, 'tall' or 'short', 'ill' or 'well' etc., etc.

Right now, in this moment, make a decision. And as you do, and you read these words, perhaps feelings of great warmth, and hope, and joy begin to flood all over you.

Record this moment – the unique moment in your life – the time, the place and, if you wish, the decision:

The premise is simple:

Your future is your choice, always.

You, me, everyone can always choose what we do, how we ACT.

And:

Whilst we may not be able to control other people, events around us and in the world, and things that happen to us, we can always control how we REACT.

So, your future is your choice, and no-one else's.

I can almost hear your objections as I write this. Objections you are raising because the idea that our future is under our own control is one of the most frightening we can ever take on board. Because, when we take it on board, we have to stop making excuses, stop giving reasons for us not being the best we already are, and we can convince anyone of this, especially ourselves.

By coaching ourselves, and others, to be the very best that we, and they, already are, and always have been.

Ask yourself this question: is there anyone on this planet, any team on this earth, any organization in the world that has achieved what you want to achieve, from a poorer, more disadvantaged starting point than you?

If the answer is yes, then your not achieving your goals/dreams/vision is your choice, and your reasoning for not doing so is an excuse. And I promise you, the answer is YES.

Now go and live.

Now go and coach.

A journey to meet your future self

Find somewhere to sit where you are comfortable and will not be disturbed. Perhaps you can put on some relaxing music or sounds of nature.

Sit up straight; put your hands in your lap or on your knees. Relax your shoulders. Let your whole body relax. Feel you are just using your bones to keep you upright and soften your muscles. Take six full, deep breaths, making the exhalation of each slightly longer each time. With each breath out, feel any tension in your body releasing.

You are going on a journey to meet your future self. The self you will be in five years' time. You are going to meet the one person who knows the right decisions for you to take, to grow more relaxed and more fulfilled and to bring more energy and enthusiasm into your life.

Imagine you are standing at the beginning of a path that leads to a beach. Perhaps the path is one you are familiar with or maybe it is a new path just for this journey. It's just a path.

Pretend you are looking around you as you start walking towards the beach. What kind of path are you walking on? Is it rough and gravelly? Is it smooth tarmac? Is it soft and sandy? What are your feet feeling as they move along the path towards the beach?

It's a beautiful day! Feel the gentle heat of the sun on your face as you walk towards the beach. There is a light wind. It is bringing the smell of the sea to you and the mixture of the heat of the sun and the gentle breeze helps you feel peaceful and relaxed, and a little excited, because today you have an appointment to meet your future self on the beach.

Look around you. Are you passing through fields? Is there a wall beside the path, or a fence, or is it just open ground? You are moving down the path towards the beach and now you feel shingle beneath your feet. You have reached the beach. Stand on the shingle for a moment and breathe in the smell of the sea. Feel the heat of the sun and the kiss of the wind on your face.

Now you are moving down the shingle beach towards the sea. Imagine the stones moving and sliding beneath your feet as you walk down the slope towards the dry sand, which leads you to the wet sand and to the sea. Feel the surface under your feet change as you step from the shingle to the dry sand. Smell the salt of the sea. Perhaps you can feel the moisture in the wind.

You are now stepping on to the wet sand. Feel the change in texture and now, just out of the reach of the breaking surf, turn right and walk beside the sea in the wet sand. Up ahead you can see a fire burning on the shingle. It is the place where you have arranged to meet your future self.

As you walk on the wet sand towards the fire, the wind carries the smell of the fire to you, the smell of wood smoke mixing with the smell of the sea. Now turn away from the sea, towards the fire, and sit down beside it, close enough to feel its gentle heat. You may be feeling excited. After all you are about to meet the one person who can tell you the right decisions to make to reach your highest potential.

As you sit there beside the fire, you become aware of someone in the distance walking towards you on the wet sand by the sea, coming from the opposite direction that you came from. As the person gets closer you start to recognize the face and the features. It is you in five years' time. You look much more relaxed than now, much healthier, and there is a confidence in your movement. Your future self grins as it approaches the fire, so pleased to see you.

Greet your future self, maybe with a hug, maybe with a kiss. Whatever feels right. Now, sit down together.

As you sit there ask your future self the questions that you would like answered.

What did you do to become so healthy?

Why do you feel much more relaxed?

What was it that made you so confident and fulfilled?

What happened in the last five years that changed so much?

Ask any of the questions in your heart and listen carefully as your future self gives you the answers. Take as long as you like …

… Soon it will be time for your future self to leave, but before it goes it wants to give you a gift to remind you of your meeting. Hold out your hand and receive the gift given to you by your future self …

… Now it is time for your future self to leave. Stand up and say goodbye. Maybe you give a last hug. Then you watch as your future self turns away and follows the wet footsteps in the sand, back to where it came from. Watch until it disappears from your view.

Now it is your time to leave. Imagine yourself walking back towards the sea and turning left to follow your old footsteps in the wet sand. Smell the sea. Feel the heat of the sun and the gentle wind on your face as you walk back down the beach. You have now reached the point where you came down to the sea, so turn left and walk across the dry sand to the shingle on your way back to the path that brought you to the beach. Feel the surface beneath your feet change as you move from the shingle to the path and walk along the path until you reach the place where you began your walk.

Now it is time to return to this time and this place. Feel your body where it touches the chair. Gently stretch your body and, when you are ready, open your eyes.

Know that, whenever you want to, you can make another appointment and go to meet your future self. Have a delicious day.

David Hill
www.businesstracks.co.uk

Journey One – Coaching from a Different Perspective – Yours

THE OBVIOUS SECRET

2

If you want something, make it big, with no Plan B. Take ownership, make a true decision and then make it happen, starting with the first action. Be inflexible on your result, and flexible on your actions to achieve it. Keep going until you achieve your dreams, and never give up, unless you choose to.

I was once introduced at a conference by a chairwoman, who said, 'And our guest speaker today is David Taylor. David has over 26 years' experience inside organizations, and today he is going share with us everything he has learned about leadership and success over that time, in just 30 minutes.'

Isn't that ridiculous! The idea that I can stretch out what little I know about leadership and success to last a complete 30 minutes.

There is only one thing I know about leadership and success, in all walks of life, and it is this: you have everything you need to be anything you want, within you, right now.

Many people, and books, will tell you that you have something missing, to be more than what you have become – I find that a very negative approach. Many others will teach you that their answers alone will make you the very best that you can be – that is more inspiring. The challenge with inspiration is that it's a bit like Chinese food: ten minutes after you have finished, you want some more.

I invite you today, right now as you read or listen to this, to take a different perspective – yours – and to be the very best, that you already are. As an individual, as a team, a project, a community or an organization, you have unique talents, gifts and potential, and when they are released, they will literally astound you.

I am often asked how I came up with this strange idea – that inside each and everyone of us, we have enough, we are enough, just as we are. And I remember exactly when and where it happened – at my son Anthony's school, when he was 13. I went in for three main reasons:

1   I wanted to put something back, into the community.
2   Anthony had never once said he wanted to be an IT Director when he grew up and I wanted to change all that!
    and
3   If you have your own children (little people in the same house), you will know that getting them to listen to you for more than a few minutes is almost impossible, so the idea of Anthony listening to me for over 30 minutes was a dream.

I was very nervous as I walked into the classroom of 35 boys, and more so when Anthony came rushing up to me and said under his breath, 'Dad, whatever you do, don't embarrass me.'

I asked, 'What do I have to do to embarrass you?'

'Anything,' he replied.

And so I started, and made my first mistake. I looked at the boys and asked them a rhetorical question:

'What, I'm wondering, will the world look like, five years from now?'

And they all put up their hands!

I had been asking that question for the previous five years of business and mind/body/spirit audiences all over the world, and no-one had ever 'answered'. I forgot, of course, that if you ask a question in a classroom, then they think you want an answer.

Moving swiftly on, I walked over to a big cupboard in the corner, took out a spade, dug a big hole, and climbed in it. Halfway through my talk, I asked the boys who would play the biggest part in their success. Which one person, above all others, will make their hopes, dreams and ambitions come true?

One boy put up his hand. I took that has a huge positive until he added the Homer Simpson expression:

'Duuuuuuuhhhhhh.'

When I asked him why he had added this, he said something that will stay with me forever. He said:

'We children get this stuff, David. It's you grown-ups that make it so complex.'

■

At a recent Parents' Evening for my eight-year-old daughter, her Form Teacher was telling my wife and me that our daughter was making good progress although she had been reluctant to tackle some of the arithmetic tasks set recently. When tackled about this, my daughter told her teacher that she couldn't find the answer to the problem – although it seemed to be more about getting started with the task than the fact that there was a problem.

Her teacher thought about this for a while and then said to my daughter, 'Why not forget about the problem and think about it as a puzzle?' – which my daughter did and promptly completed the task. By reframing what the issue is, and thinking about it in another way, it obviously allowed my daughter to tackle the task confidently.

In management there are seldom many clear-cut situations – just shades of grey with different choices. Considering issues as puzzles, rather than problems, can lead to individuals and teams generating lots of different potential solutions – all of which may be valid.

Rob Ferrari

■

'We children get this stuff, David. It's you grown-ups that make it so complex.'

■

After that, it was all about recovery. I thought I did OK, and concluded with the statement that I had made to many audiences before:

'What is absolutely wonderful, fantastic, about being alive today, is that no-one really knows what is going to happen next.'

There was a pause, and then another boy put up his hand and said:

'I know what's going to happen next, Sir. We've got double French.'

I felt about two-feet tall, and as I drove away from the school, I laughed to myself:

'Can you imagine, with all of the challenges we have in our lives – in our personal lives, in our careers, in the world – if we could take such control over what happens next?' And then it came to me.

We can. When we look within. When we awaken what we already have, within ourselves, within our organizations. When we realize that we are enough, just as we are.

'We children get this stuff, David.' Yes, they do, and so did we, once. And we can, once again. If we so choose.

Because you, and only you, can choose your life.

On the day you were born, naked, you had everything you needed, to be anything you wanted. On the day that you die, naked, you will look back on whether you achieved everything that you could have. If all of this comes down to one thing, it is about fulfilling the promise of your first few seconds, while ensuring no regrets in your last …

When you were born, naked, you only had two fears – a fear of falling over, and a fear of loud noises. Any other fear that you have is separate from you, like 'the Emperor's New Clothes'.

Everything you need, to be anything you want, you already have within you, just as you are.

■

Many others will tell you to be more than what you have become;

Many people will inspire you to be the very best that you can be;

I invite you to be the very best that you already are.

■

Your truth, integrity and authenticity come from deep within, and your success will come from removing those false, limiting beliefs, those 'Emperor's New Clothes', that separate you from the essence of who you truly are, and always have been.

It is this separation, from what you feel now to who you truly are, that is the root cause of any and all anxieties, worries and fears that you may have. When you accept that, you start to move towards your major premise – your underlying belief system. Just reading this, and believing whatever you believe, is sometimes enough to bring you an inner peace and joy that reconnects you with your inner power.

In your life, your success has not happened by accident. It has come as a result of your following a specific process, an exact formula. You have the right to know this formula, and when you apply it knowingly, your success will be inevitable. It is powerful, and the results are amazing.

■

The Formula for Guaranteed Success (tell everyone you know, destroy the mystery and hype surrounding business success, and *leadership*, **forever**)
- *Know where you want to go/be*: the WHAT – Dreams and Outcomes
- *Know where you are now*: the YOU – Ownership and Honesty
- *Know what you have to do, to get to where you want to go/be*: the MOMENT – Choices and True Decisions
- *Do it!*: the First Action – the HOW – Action and Persistence

■

Navigating the Formula

Know where you want to go/be: the WHAT – Dreams and Outcomes

Have massive dreams – a very logical, left-brain thing to do. Think of what you could achieve, and double it. Ask yourself, has anyone in more difficult circumstances than you or your team achieved what you want to achieve? If so (and the answer is that they have) then you can achieve it as well. If no one has ever achieved what you want to achieve, what an opportunity … And, by the way, when you do achieve your dream, it will be those very same people that said 'you can't' that will be the first to say they always knew you would …

Know where you are now: the YOU – Ownership and Honesty

You are either in ownership, or you are not. In your 'team', would you ever say anything about another team member behind their back that you would not say to their face? If so, you are not in ownership of your life. Also, you are not the 'finished article'. That will only happen when you are in a box and not breathing. So accept that you are you, and be honest about your natural gifts and talents and what you bring to the world (and remember what nice things others will say about you at your funeral).

Know what you have to do, to get to where you want to go/be: the MOMENT – Choices and True Decisions

Make a true decision – decide what you want to achieve, or who you want to be, and close off ALL other possibilities. It only takes a heartbeat.

Do it!: the First Action – The HOW – Action and Persistence

Take one action. Then ask yourself the only question you need to ask – does this action, this behaviour, this thought, take me closer to where I want to go, or who I want to be? If yes, do more of the same … If not, do something else …

And now, celebrate. Share your decision with a loved one, have a glass of champagne (or water!) or simply smile (everyone else will wonder what you are smiling about).

You will read many books that will tell you that making such a decision is enough – that you need to do no more. Such books are very inspiring, and focus on positive thinking.

Not this one. Quite apart from the fact it would be the shortest book in history, there is one other thing that you must do, and always have done, when your life has been transformed. Positive thinking is itself hugely liberating, and making such a decision takes you much, much closer to your new 'reality'. And it is absolutely worthless, without something else.

Right now, imagine your biggest dream, your greatest hope, your wildest ambition – and make it huge. Close your eyes as you picture it, hear it, and feel it *as if* it was happening right now.

Now open your eyes, has anything changed? Yes, you feel differently, you have a new energy and a stronger belief that you will achieve it. First, though, you must do something.

▪

You must do something.

▪

When I say 'must', of course I do not mean that you have to, you don't have to do anything. I only mean that, if there is something you want to change in your life or choose in your life or help others to do the same, doing nothing won't deliver.

So, take action. Just one, to start with – perhaps a small step, maybe a huge leap. To make your dreams come true, and help others to do the same. To transform a project or a team. To lead your organization to levels that others would describe as 'impossible'.

And that is what this book is about. Taking action.

Yes, dream, discover and decide. And *do something about it*.

That is the difference between thinking about the adventure of your life, and actually being on that adventure. And that is what this book is all about. Read it as you wish, agree with what you choose, and please, please write all over it.

▪

In Athens, I had the great honour to share a platform with some of the top motivational speakers in the world, including Michael Breen and Jack Canfield. Needless to say, they had inspired the global audience of 150 business leaders to the rooftops.

When I stood up to do my session, I asked how inspired everyone was. People responded pretty much according to culture – the South Americans yelled and screamed, the Italians and South Africans clapped and shouted, the Europeans nodded politely and smiled.

I asked them how much they were inspired – from zero to ten – the average in that room was 12! It was pure energy, a hothouse of power. So the next words I said rather surprised the audience:

'Inspired to do what?' I asked.

Silence. The energy and motivation stayed where it was, it did not leave the room, it just sat there, waiting, as inspiration always does – waiting for a focus, a direction, an action, on which to apply its power.

■

Inspired to do what?

We spend so much time ***talking*** action and not enough ***taking*** action. We meet and chat and discuss and analyse what we should or should not do – we even have business events and round-table dinners to do this. And we all get together and put forward our points of view and experiences and hear others' points of view and experiences.

And then what?

At best we are inspired.

To do what?

■

If there is something, anything that you want to change in your life, then make a decision and do something about it. This book will contain hundreds of ideas; if they take you closer to achieving your dream, then do more of the same, if they take you further away, then do something else …

And if that doesn't work, then do something else
And if that doesn't work, then do something else
And if that doesn't work, then do something else
And if that doesn't work, then do something else
And if that doesn't work, then do something else
And if that doesn't work, then do something else
And if that doesn't work, then do something else
And if that doesn't work, then do something else
And if that doesn't work, then do something else
And if that doesn't work, then do something else
And if that doesn't work, then do something else
And if that doesn't work, then do something else
And if that doesn't work, then do something else
And if that doesn't work, then do something else
And if that doesn't work, then do something else
And if that doesn't work, *then do something else*
And if that doesn't work, *then do something else*
And if that doesn't work, *then do something else*
And if that doesn't work, *then do something else*

And if that doesn't work, ***then do something else***
And if that doesn't work, ***then do something else***
And if that doesn't work, ***then do something else***
And if that doesn't work, ***then do something else***
And if that doesn't work, ***then do something else***
And if that doesn't work, ***then do something else***
And then go to bed

And when you wake up in the morning, check you have a pulse, and if you do, rejoice, then take action:

And if that doesn't work, then do something else
And if that doesn't work, then do something else
And if that doesn't work, then do something else
And if that doesn't work, then do something else
And if that doesn't work, then do something else
And if that doesn't work, then do something else
And if that doesn't work, then do something else
And if that doesn't work, then do something else
And if that doesn't work, then do something else
And if that doesn't work, then do something else
And if that doesn't work, then do something else
And if that doesn't work, then do something else
And if that doesn't work, then do something else
And if that doesn't work, then do something else
And if that doesn't work, *then do something else*
And if that doesn't work, *then do something else*
And if that doesn't work, *then do something else*
And if that doesn't work, *then do something else*
And if that doesn't work, ***then do something else***
And if that doesn't work, ***then do something else***
And if that doesn't work, ***then do something else***
And if that doesn't work, ***then do something else***
Or give up

▪

And giving up is the norm. Keeping going when all around have given up is one of the lost golden wonders. Some people are rejected so often as they grow up, they learn to fear it, and do everything they can to avoid it. Others are rejected so often as they grow up, they learn to fear it, and decide instead to love it – and when rejection happens, they truly love it, as it is a sure sign that success is on the way.

And what about in the first place – how daring are we, as grown-ups?

■

Genuine university entrance examination question: 'What is courage?'
One student wrote: 'This is.'
And walked out.
And got in.

■

Imagine if we lacked persistence in our everyday lives. Next time we are walking along a pavement, pretending to be a child again:

'If I can avoid the cracks, I'll be fine.'
and
'If I can just walk 10 steps with my eyes closed, there will be peace in the world.'

And then you fall over – and of course instead of getting up again, brushing yourself down and walking quickly away, you would say to yourself:

'I'm not getting up, I might fall over again. No way. No, I'll just lie here for a while … '

Like when we ask our children what they did at school today.

And, by the way, my time at schools and with children has taught me that there is a global conspiracy, by children, to answer that question in a precise and particular way every time. It is the only story I keep exactly the same wherever I speak, in the world.

You know how the conversation goes …

■

Parent: 'What did you do at school today?'
Child: 'Nothing.'
At this point, parent remembers what they teach you on one of those How to Communicate with your Child courses:
Parent (louder): 'What did you do at school today?'
Child (louder): 'Nothing.'
Parent (louder, closer and s-l-o-w-e-r): 'Whaat diiid yooou dooooooo aaaaaaaat schoooooool tooodayyyyyyyyy?'
Child: 'Noooooooottttttthhhhhhhhhhiiiiiiiinnnnnnnggggg.'
And storms upstairs.

■

After two years of personal experience of this one, I decided to do something about it. I was speaking to a school in London, and the interaction went as follows:

■

'What question do your parents ask you that really annoys you?'

Whole school, in unison: 'What did we do at school today?'

'And how do you answer that question?'

'Nothing.'

By this stage, the children all think this is great fun. The teachers split into two camps – half are amused and dare not show it; the other half are mentally deciding that David Taylor will never, ever darken their school doors again.

And then I ask the children:

'Would you like them never to ask that question again?'

'**YES PLEASE.**' – school roof nearly comes off.

'OK.' I now have to shout above the excitement. 'Next time they ask, tell them.'

Near silence as this sinks in – a few giggles break out, which turn to hysteria when I add:

'They don't want to know – they are just being polite.'

And then I add, 'Besides, they haven't got the time.'

■

So, the next time you ask your child what they have done at school today, and they tell you, they tell you every single detail, and it lasts two hours plus, you know the secret's out. My best advice then is this: when they finish, and ask you what you did today, at the office, or work, or wherever, simply reply, 'Nothing'.

■

Meantime, if they say 'Nothing', what can you do?

Ask a different question.

And if that doesn't work?

Ask a different question.

And if that doesn't work?

Ask a different question.

And if that doesn't work?

Ask a different question.

And if that doesn't work?

■

It's like being stuck in a maze. The way out of any maze is to do something different, and if that doesn't work, do something different, and keep doing different things until you move closer to where you want to go, or who you want to be.

And in doing this, we discover what children know only too well. The wonder of persistence and bravery – the two go hand-in-hand.

At this point, it is the fathers who often put up their hands and say they don't let their children use persistence to get the better of them.

Come Onnnnnnnnnnnnnnnnn!

■

Scene: An ice cream van, summertime
Characters: A dad and his daughter/son
Act One – Scene One
Child: 'I want an ice cream.'
Dad: 'No, you've eaten quite enough for today.'
Child: 'I want an ice cream.'
Dad: 'No, I've told you – and besides, lunch is in an hour.'
Child: 'I want an ice cream.'
Dad: 'All right, but don't tell your mum.'

■

Journey One – Coaching from a Different Perspective –Yours

THE DEAL, THE DECISION AND THE DAY-TO-DAY

Too many training courses and company events end on a real high, and then nothing happens. I believe this is for three reasons:

1 Because people attend these events to find out more knowledge or information than they already have – which is a waste of time, for two reasons. Firstly, they already 'know' all of what they need to know to make a difference and, secondly, they are still out there looking for the 'perfect' answer, which does not exist. If it is information and knowledge that people need, they need not attend these events: they just need to go to a search engine.

2 Because people will most often focus on what they do not want, rather than what they do. This not only causes a mental blockage to accepting what they do want (and will lead them to endless discussion and debate that other people are 'wrong', even though they have not found out what is 'right'), it also causes them to automatically move towards what they do not want, because they keep thinking and talking about it. Remember, as human beings we automatically move in the direction of our most dominant thoughts.

3 Because they do not commit (make a true decision) to actually doing something – to taking action that relates to something that is important to them.

You can overcome these three reasons in a very simple way, through The Deal. It goes like this:

You have a choice: we can debate and discuss, and then debate and discuss some more … or we can actually do something. So, for key decisions and actions, I will tell you exactly what to do, and you will do what I suggest, *or you will do something else* – you will actually commit to doing something, as opposed to doing nothing.

This – along with there being no 'right' or 'wrong', there only being what serves you (takes you closer to your desired result) or what does not serve you (takes you further away) – removes people's excuses, ends the debate and leads to action.

Outcome: everyone agrees that this event or action is about making a big difference, not talking about making a big difference.

The Deal

I promise to share with you the most powerful, exact ways to achieve what you want to achieve.

And in return …

… you promise to take action.

And that action may be what I suggest, or, if you disagree with something I suggest, you will do something else – *you will do something*.

Whether it is something I suggested, or the complete opposite, that's fine. I do not mind if you believe in me, I want to know if you believe in you.

OK – You probably read that last bit, you took it in, now please re-read it.

The Deal

I promise to share with you the most powerful, exact ways to achieve what you want to achieve.

And in return …

… you promise to take action.

And that action may be what I suggest, or, if you disagree with something I suggest, you will do something else – *you will do something*.

Whether it is something I suggested, or the complete opposite, that's fine. I do not mind if you believe in me, I want to know if you believe in you.

Decide to do The Deal.

Or give this book to someone else, someone who will.

Maybe you thought 'OK, I will do the deal, later' ...

If not now, then **when?**

Imagine if everything you have ever done, all that you have ever known, and each thought you have ever had, comes down to this very moment. As you read this.

How powerful would that be? Not tomorrow, not next week, not next year. Right now.

If everything you have ever been, every choice you have ever made, and each action you have ever taken, came together in this very moment. As you read this, wherever you are in the world. Right now. Because they do.

▪

Welcome to the adventure of your lifetime.

▪

And that is not meant to be *thought-provoking*, it is written to be *action-provoking*.

Please, wherever you are, whenever you are reading this, and whoever you are, stop reading right now, and look at the time. Remember it or, ideally, write it down here – the exact time, day, month and year.

The Time is Now:

The Day:

The Month:

The Year:

Now, think about that moment. There will never be another exact time like that in your lifetime, or in the history of the world. Ten years from now, ten thousand years from now, that time you have written on this page will still be totally, and absolutely unique. And all you have to decide is whether you take control of that moment in time, or let it have control over you.

■

> The *now* is all we have – so, in this very *now,* what are you, personally, going to do?

■

Not yesterday, or tomorrow – right now. For it is the actions we take *right now* that will make all the difference. This is not easy, as our minds so often drift into our pasts, and our futures ...

We understand living and acting in the moment. Logically, however, that is not enough – because just as we convince our left brain that this is really quite a good idea, that moment is gone, and then the next one and so on. It is like an escalator (up or down) – which step will you join? Which moment will you choose to leap on board?

Take another look at that unique time, that single moment in history that you wrote down. Not only has it now passed, so have many others between then and now.

All those single, unique moments, chances, opportunities, gone forever. How depressing is that?

Still, think of all the other chances, opportunities, yet to come. How exciting is that?

Until that last one – those final few moments that we have on this planet.

Because they are getting closer all the time.

If we could transport ourselves through time to that very moment, what would we be thinking about in that last moment?

'I wonder what people will think about me, after I have died?'

'I wish I had spent more time (insert your words here).'

or:

'I feel I did my best in life, and helped other people along the way.'

Of course, the greatest challenge is that, chances are, you will never know when that moment will happen.

The Decision

> We always overestimate what we can achieve in a year, and we always underestimate what we can achieve in a moment.

■

Living in the moment is our first big challenge; our second is making a true decision in that moment (a decision that you will actually keep to, and make happen). With this, we can sometimes feel that the moment has to be very important – as if some moments in time are more significant than others.

After all, don't these *life-choosing moments* only happen at particular times, such as when we reach a certain age (life begins at 40), at the start of a New Year or Millennium? Of course they do, if you so choose. If you want to wait until next first of January to choose your life, fine (although you may not be around); if you want to wait around until the next moment … which is now here … then make a *life-choosing* decision.

Not a life-*changing* decision. Those are very frequent and happen each and every day – made by default, by other people on our behalf, made by our skin cells, our bone cells, and other parts of our body just to keep us alive.

A life-choosing decision.

How long are you going to wait? What is it about our possible futures that stop you doing what you most want to do, now?

When we look at newborn babies we often say to ourselves, or even out loud, 'Isn't it wonderful? They have their whole life ahead of them.' Well, so do you, whoever you are, wherever you are, and whatever your age.Or should you delay your decision, to say, Wednesday, 3 February 2100?

The Day-to-Day

I once went on a fantastic team-building weekend. One of those outward-bound courses. On the Sunday morning we went canoeing, and I discovered something I was a natural at. It was so inspiring to be in there, on the water. It was an experience I will never forget.

The following day I was in work, on a real high, when we had a crisis with our computer system. The team that had only 24 hours earlier been at one began to split. It got unpleasant, nasty even. I reminded them of the experience we had shared on the water, to which someone said, 'Yes, and there is never a canoe around when you really need one.'

Mike Antrim

■

It is all very well learning how to coach, how to be successful, how to be a leader, how to help others; however, if we do not know how to make it happen in a real day-to-day situation, it is close to being a waste of time.

That is why the day-to-day is so critical. It is the only way to move beyond ideas and theory, and into action. Because it gives relevance, a context to our lives – and if we do not have that, what we know is meaningless.

Think back to your school. Now ask yourself this – how much of what I learned at school, am I really applying in my life right now?

How much was relevant to your world today? There was one thing you did learn at school that was very relevant – you learned what you were good at, and what you were not. You learned if you were good at languages, at maths, at history. And more often than not, that 'learning' has stayed with you – that is the most powerful context because it applies in all of your life.

And within these general beliefs, we have your own, specific, exact reality – the life you are leading right now, the project you are working on today, the team you are a part of.

Unless what is written in this book can be applied to those, what is written here is pointless.

You may have been on a leadership course where you debated the difference between leadership and management.

So what?

You may have listened to a speaker who has achieved an amazing feat, such as climbing a mountain under very difficult circumstances.

So what?

Unless their experiences can be directly related to your day-to-day dreams and challenges.

And we are all bombarded with so much information, and knowledge, and data – more in one day than most people had in their whole lifetime 100 years ago.

So what?

Unless we can know which information can be applied to ourselves, right now.

So what?

So, throughout this book, as you coach yourself and others, make sure each and every example is real – a real day-to-day issue, challenge or dream. What are you going to do, in your life, your job, your reality, with who you are, what you have and the hundred of 'How To's in this book?

Next time you have a great, huge and massive dream, ask yourself three questions:

One – Is this logical?

Yes, because it takes exactly the same time, energy and brainpower to have a massive dream, as it does to have a small one

Two – How do I know it is big enough?

By the number of detractors. You will have no shortage of critics and detractors. The more powerful your idea, the more detractors you will have. Rejoice in knowing it will be these very people who, when you achieve your dream, will come to you and say, 'I always knew you would do it.'

Three – How does it help other people achieve their dreams?

We will always need other people to help us achieve our dream, and it helps massively if, in the process, we can help them achieve theirs. Not only do we have automatic energy and mutual encouragement, we also have flow. Flow is where we are in tune with others, and with life.

And The Naked Coach is about you making a difference for yourself, and for other people.

Journey One – Coaching from a Different Perspective – Yours

HIT OR MYTH?

4

Hit

Everything you really need to know about business coaching in a single page (this one)

■

What is business coaching?

Any and every intervention that enables people, teams and organizations to be their very best.

(There are many other choices of answer – so many that your head will start to hurt, not one of the desired outcomes of coaching. See 'Myth?', starting on page 47.)

■

At 18, I decided to pursue a career with HSBC. I set myself the following goals and wrote myself a letter to remind me:

- Drive a car by 20 – achieved by 19
- Be Assistant Manager by 21 – achieved by 20
- Buy my first house by 21 – achieved by 19
- Be Branch Manager by 23 – achieved by 21

I set goals, believe in myself, strategize how to achieve, visualize myself achieving, challenge myself with succeeding and making my dreams reality. This has been the key to my success.

Key advice given to me to succeed:

- Chandra Vadivale (father & teacher) has taught me to believe and have faith in God and myself.
- Sandy Jegasundaram (life partner & mentor) inspired me to think, : 'I don't care what others think about me, because I know my path and I am excellent at it. This excellence will show via MY service and happiness.'
- Laura Pescott (manager & role model) – 'Never under estimate yourself.'

What's the difference between 'Business' and 'Life' Coaching? Business is simply where it happens.

Divya L Vadivale

■

What benefits do people gain from being coached?

They achieve success, by their own definition, faster, because they are being guided, helped, supported and valued.

What benefits do organizations gain from coaching?

They achieve success, by their own definition, faster, because their people are being guided, helped, supported and valued.

Why would people choose to be a business coach?

Because it helps other people, helps yourself in the process, adds value to lives and organizations, and we would all want to be remembered for the good we have done.

Are there any codes of behaviour in coaching?

Yes. There are so many standards that if you gathered them all together, they would fill a truck.

The key ones are integrity, confidentiality and respect for each other.

Myth?

> They are not true (unless you want them to be, in which case they are).
>
> ■

1 Business coaching is about the process, not the person

Business coaching has become a worldwide industry, its awareness and importance is growing, and its popularity rising. All good news, you would think – yet also a problem, because as it becomes an industry in its own right, so it develops its own jargon and complexities.

Also, with so many coaches around, everyone is marketing what makes them unique and different and why you and others should choose them in particular. Again, although competition is great, it can make it all fragmented and a little confusing.

Please, however you approach business coaching, know that it always comes down to one thing – the *person* being coached.

Business coaching is about you, not about a maze of meanings … but that said, what is the difference between 'coaching' and 'mentoring'?

2 The maze of meanings

In the worlds of leadership and success, the hunt for definitions continues apace. Indeed, 'leadership' and 'success' have many different definitions in themselves.

'Coaching' is no exception. For this book I asked 20 business coaches to define for me what they do. I received 20 different answers, many of which contradicted each other!

So I decided to ask for some different definitions – have some fun, do the same. These are the 'clearest' answers I received:

▪

What is 'coaching'? – helping and guiding others through facilitation.

What is 'facilitation'? – bringing out the best in others, through help, guidance and counselling.

What is 'counselling'? – listening to others, their problems and supporting them.

What is 'supporting'? – ensuring people have what they need and supervising properly.

What is 'supervising'? – leading and managing and training.

What is 'training'? – assisting others to gain new skills and knowledge through teaching and advising.

What is 'advising'? – suggesting possible courses of action to achieve a given result based on your own experience, and perhaps through consulting.

What is 'consulting'? – helping people and teams by asking questions, and perhaps through mentoring an organization.

What is 'mentoring'? – acting as a role model and guiding others.

What is 'guiding'? – being a coach.

▪

Round and round we go, and where we stop, nobody knows.

The term 'coaching' is becoming prevalent in all areas of life and business, and yet it is a term that has no specific, agreed definition. In addition, other oft-used terms carry similar confusion, most notably 'mentoring', 'facilitation', and 'training'. Deeper confusion is caused by each of these terms being defined even further. For example, in coaching we have 'directive' and 'non-directive'.

It is absolutely critical now to give definitive, seminal definitions of coaching and these other areas that are clear, concise and compelling, in all their forms and applications, across both business and personal agendas; a definition that everyone can use, that moves beyond the debate in every other area of personal development, to an agenda of action and results.

So, it is time for a definitive definition:

▪

Business coaching is any and every intervention that enables people, teams and organizations to be their very best.

▪

I am suggesting 'coaching' as a catch-all for any and every intervention – personal and online – that enables people to be the very best.

In this definition, coaches are able to adapt, and switch their approaches and interventions according to the needs of their partner – the person they are working with. So, one moment they may be 'facilitating' and then they may be 'training' and then they may be 'mentoring,' all in the space of five minutes (this is covered more in Myth 5, 'The Place of Power', below).

While we can debate the meaning of what we call what we are doing, we can delay and avoid addressing why we are doing it. No longer – the name game stops here.

Let's cut through the myth of meanings or the myth of relevance – call it whatever you wish, the name for the help is of no importance compared to the help itself, and the impact of that help.

So, that is coaching defined, and if you don't agree with me, great, what is your definition? Just make sure you come up with one that enables you to do it, and not just talk about doing it. If we do not, we simply enter the world of business jargon:

▪

Business jargon is everywhere, and with clarity, focus and simplicity as three key aims for success in the 21st century, we must do something about it.

Jargon happens on three levels – generally adopted/accepted phrases and words that run across different organizations, such as initiatives (Right First Time), phrases taken from books (Good to Great), and other terms that come from I know not where (Best Practice).

I write this with some caution – the Naked Leader philosophy is to keep things very simple, not least because I only understand simple – and yet I have been accused of inventing my own jargon around simplicity.

Also, I spent many years in Information Technology and so am as 'guilty' as anyone else of using jargon and accepting it as part of the everyday lexicon. The first term I heard when I went into telecoms was 'twisted pair' (don't ask). I well remember being told with absolute disdain by a consultant that 'knowledge management' was 'the management of knowledge', and my personal favourite, although I have never met one, is a 'thin client'!

Another personal favourite is the services company, who helpfully explain on their website what they do:

'Cartus' customized solutions boost employee productivity and satisfaction, while supporting effective program management and cost control. Our focus on service excellence, technology investment, and Six Sigma measurement standards ensures consistent results-driven performance. Clients receive continual information on best practices, cost-reduction opportunities, and competitive program enhancements, while our consultants provide each employee with resourceful and responsive personal advocacy.'

As *The Economist* puts it:

'This is a sort of über-jargon, expressed in such an Orwellian, dead-pan tone that it is not even funny.'

So, where do we draw the line?

Well, you draw the line the moment you hear a term, word, phrase or acronym (usually a TLA – Three Letter Acronym), that you do not understand, or, and here's the rub, that you feel anyone else in the room does not understand.

This takes bravery. However, as with so much bravery, it will make you a hero. And remember, while the person using the jargon thinks they are being clever, in fact they are being and looking very, very stupid.

Whether it is you that does not understand, or you feel someone else present may not do so, simply ask what they mean.

If the person using the jargon laughs, or scoffs, or says something like 'I thought everyone knows what that means', look them right in the eyes and, if you feel confrontational, say:

'Apparently not'.

Or you may go for the gentler:

'I don't. Would you mind explaining?'

You are speaking on behalf of the silent majority, and will win massive respect.

Remember:

Organizations are simply legal collections of people, so it is people who invent, use and thrive on jargon.

Never ever use jargon with a customer – and if they pull you up on a term, explain it. If they use jargon, ask them what they mean.

People who use jargon are doing it to look clever, when in fact they make themselves look the complete opposite

People who use jargon a lot do it to make themselves indispensable, which is the fastest route to redundancy that I have ever known.

With CAL*

* clarity and love

■

3 The paradox myth: anyone can be a coach; not everyone can be a coach, and yet everyone already is.

■

A friend of mine smoked over 30 cigarettes a day, and when he went for a health check, the nurse he met told him in no uncertain terms how dangerous this was to his health. This nurse was overweight, very overweight, and my friend could not take what she said seriously, because if she could not sort herself out, what right did she have to tell him what to do? As if this nurse's weight had anything to do with his own health.

■

We all do this at a sub-conscious level; when we are told to do something, or are advised by another, we will ask ourselves what right do they have to help us – and this question blocks the power of the message itself.

And so, everyone wants to give us help, advice and guidance.

And so, everyone is a coach.

What determines whether we take that advice on board? Looking at the smoking advice example – the nurse was qualified to give advice, however my friend did not take it on board, because she was clearly *not applying it to herself*. People have the same attitude towards coaching and life-changing principles – if they do not believe them, they do not take them on board.

Take NLP – Neuro Linguistic Programming.

On the one hand: 'NLP is a very powerful analysis of who and how we are, and a group of powerful tools that help us and others to live our lives to the maximum while being in rapport with others. It cuts through the complexities of academic psychology and was originally designed and developed by Richard Bandler and John Grinder.' People who believe this use NLP every day to help themselves and their organizations.

On the other: 'NLP is simply a collection of the obvious – public domain material wrapped up in shiny jargon that confuses others by telling them what they thought they already knew. It is an over-simplification of the realities of academic psychology and is little more than a commercial rip-off from the works of Milton Eriksson.' People who believe this do not use NLP any day to help themselves and their organizations.

Which of these is 'right'? Whichever you believe.

And that is the key, the paradox, and too often the excuse. We have to believe the person, or the philosophy, or the whatever. And if we don't, we will not be sufficiently open-minded to take it on board.

So, if you do not believe in yourself, you are unlikely to listen to your own best advice (i.e. ideas that will take you forward). And it is exactly the same with business coaching.

OK – let's resolve the paradox:

When you are 'given' advice and guidance – ask yourself not who or where it is from, simply ask yourself this: 'Does this information serve me, or my team or organization, or not?', even if you have not necessarily lived through that advice before.

For me, the power of coaching is all about challenging the proposition that powerful learning can only come from experience and therefore that you have to make your own mistakes in life. I think what sits behind this is the perceived notion that you can't be told the answer … or rather that you can, but it has no lasting impact unless it comes from within your own set of experiences.

Simon La Fosse

Then you may ask yourself – 'Do I agree with that advice?' That question will tend to be asked, based on the person giving you the advice, and whether they put that advice into practice, in their own life.

And this is critical if you want to help others as a coach. Because the impact of our coaching is in both what we say, *and* what we do. Which is more important and influential? What we do, every time.

Why is what we do, our action, more powerful than what we say when it comes to influencing and leading others? An action shows commitment to what you believe is the right direction in life. An action shows that we say what we mean – and will do something about it.

Saying something is like scientific theory; it's an unproven idea.

Doing something is like scientific fact – it shows you that it is possible and repeatable.

What we do influences people more because actions create reactions. It is not mandatory. However, if you want to gain fast-track credibility as a business coach, match what you say with what you do, and how you live:

So when you ask other people to do something, would you do it yourself?

When you advise someone to do something, would that include yourself?

When you coach someone to do something, have you done it yourself?

I was asked one of the most unexpected, left-field questions ever. I was on a table with four people, three of whom were excitedly debating leadership. Then, during a pause, the fourth person, who had not said a single word until that moment, looked up from his food and asked me simply:

'Do you really believe – I mean, really believe, what you say?'

The table went quiet. Those who know me will testify that I rarely use one word when twenty will do, and so I was ready to launch into a long answer about passion, belief and values, all supported with examples and case studies. However, this time my heart took over, and I looked the questioner in the eyes, deep into his eyes, and said simply: 'Yes.'

To which he said: 'In that case – thank you.'

I learned something very powerful in that hotel restaurant – that when one is presenting, yes, the audience is thinking, 'What's in it for me?' and 'How can I apply what the presenter is saying in my life or to help others?' but, more than these two, they are asking themselves, 'Does this person really believe what they are saying?'

And when the answer is 'yes', then the speaker is not only being more persuasive and having greater impact, they are also simply being themselves.

■

4 Mind mastery

Traditional and academic psychology focuses on how our minds work – why we do what we do. Inevitably, this is often expressed using terms and language that few people understand. The challenge for academic psychologists is to make a very complex area, still not fully explored or understood, accessible to all.

The ideal mind-mastery practitioner will know a little about how the mind works, and be able to explain this in simple language that is clear, concise and compelling (i.e. relevant). They will have a focus on results; and above all they will have a kitbag of expertise and tools they can call on to achieve those results, depending on the needs of the person they are working with.

In sports, they will also be expert at the particular game they coach, e.g. golf. This is absolutely critical, because they will be in the world of the golfer, and not in the world of psychology. Overall, this places the power not with them, but rather with the golfer seeking peak performance on demand. When the power is with the golfer, they have the choices, they have the ability to replicate perfect shots whenever they choose, and transformation is achieved, very, very fast. Such practitioners, Naked Coaches, enable people to be the very best that they already are.

How can we do otherwise?

Naked Coaches believe it is everyone's birthright to be successful, and to know how to achieve it so that they can help others. Naked Coaches do not judge other experts or masters in the personal development arena, no matter how much we are criticized, as we often are, for making mind and performance mastery too simple, available to too many people, and for achieving results too fast.

At the end of everything, out of this whole, complex area known as mind mastery, the Naked Coach approach is interested in one thing above all else – rapid results that enable people to rekindle the powers they already have, to remember who they really are, and to return to being themselves. Rapid, repeatable, measurable and sustainable results that can be obtained whenever the person or team so choose.

5   The place of power

The power in any coaching relationship must be with the person being coached, not with the coach (it is different if you go to a dentist, where you trust them to do the job that they can identify needs to be done).

Often in the 'coaching' world, people specialize in one discipline or another – so we have people who are coaches, others who may be mentors and others as trainers. This gives rise to a fundamental problem that must be overcome if any clear definition of coaching is going to work.

Specialists who are mentors will carry out a mentoring session, and if they feel their 'client' can benefit from coaching, they may arrange a separate session with a coach, and so on. For this reason, many business leaders have several people working with them – one coach, one mentor and perhaps a facilitator they call in when required.

This situation, born out of the personal development industry, is ridiculous, expensive, confusing and expensive. And, here's the rub – it also places the power and authority with the person providing the mentoring/coaching/training, etc. rather than the way it should be, with the 'client'.

■

Naked Coaching is different, and is defined as being any and every intervention that enables people, teams and business to be their very best.

■

Naked Coaches are able to adapt and switch from their approaches and interventions according to the needs of their partner – the person they are working with. So, one moment they may be 'facilitating' and then they may be 'training' and then they may be 'mentoring', all in the space of five minutes.

6 Personality types … when used as an excuse for the way we are …

We are all fascinated by our favourite subject, ourselves. That is not 'selfish', it is not 'big-headed', it simply is. And has to be.

As the one thing we are masters at, absolute geniuses at being, is ourselves. No-one else can do it quite like we can. So we, quite naturally, want to learn about ourselves – our strengths, our weaknesses, our personality types.

We answer a series of questions, and may discover that we are an Introvert, not an Extrovert, and perhaps that we are Logical, more than Emotional. These things are fascinating to discover, as long as we appreciate that the conclusions can be changed. Indeed, every personality- and team-type questionnaire makes it clear that they are only taking a mental photograph at a single point in time in your life.

And therein lies their power, and their danger.

The power is that once we have discovered we are, say, an Introvert, that is only how we feel at that moment and we can choose to change that. Otherwise a test we do at age five will give us exactly the same results at age fifty, which is clearly not the case. Our learning, experience and conditioning between five and fifty lead to the different result.

The danger is that we may believe that being an Introvert is 'us', and that we can do nothing about it, and we start to behave accordingly. Perhaps worse, if that behaviour does not help us or our organizations, we can use the results of the personality test as an excuse for our behaviour, as if that behaviour is not under our own control.

I believe that criticism of personality tests is very unfair – they are proven, well thought-through and established. It is the interpretation of the results that is critical.

In fact, coaching sessions carried out after the completion of such a test can be very powerful, as someone may wish to change a result, by choosing a different behaviour.

I am a fan of using personality types, in particular those that measure discretionary effort – how much a person chooses to give in terms of effort, belief and making things happen. One of the most important theories I learned at college was Marginal Propensity to Consume (MPC). Forgive the jargon; your MPC measures how much effort and energy you will invest to obtain a specific result. If you want to buy something, how much effort will you go to, to obtain it? Would you walk to the shops? Would you buy it from another country online and have it imported?, etc. This can be translated into the worlds of coaching and success – and for me, this is most powerful way to use personality types.

Q: Because you, and only you, can choose your life ... what life do you choose?

It is not our abilities that show who we truly are, it is our choices.

Professor Dumbledore
(From Harry Potter and the Chamber of Secrets *– Film)*
Original Book by J.K.Rowling
Screenplay by Steven Kloves

Q: Imagine life as a corridor with an infinite number of doors

... and the doors are your choices – now, in your mind walk down the corridor – what is written on the doors?

(With thanks to Tony Rhymer)

■

I feel strongly that creating a climate where alternative possibilities and new realities become more real for people is a key part of coaching.

Dr Mark Durkin
Head of School for Marketing and Entrepreneurship
University of Ulster, Belfast, Northern Ireland

■

Now, which of those doors are you going to open, and walk through? It is time to decide what you *want* in life, and move away from what you *don't*.

■

Anyone can oppose – it's fun to be against things,
and there comes a time when you have to be for things as
well.

The Libertine (Screenplay by Stephen Jeffreys)

■

Q: Imagine if you simply could not fail:

    What would you do?
    Where would you go?
    Who would you be?

■

Alice laughed: 'There's no use trying' she said. 'One can't believe impossible things.' 'I daresay you haven't had much practice,'' said the Queen. 'When I was younger, I always did it for half an hour a day. Why, sometimes I've believed as many as six impossible things before breakfast.'
Through the Looking Glass, Lewis Carroll

■

Q: What are your strengths/gifts/talents?
(Please do not leave this page blank!)

It is easy to be cynical – it is far more rewarding to take action.

Q: If you could ask yourself one question, what would it be?

I don't mind if you don't believe in me, I want to know if you believe in you.

Journey Two

*Self-Coaching – Applying
The Formula to You*

Journey Two – Self-Coaching – Applying The Formula to You

KNOW WHERE YOU WANT TO GO

This Journey is on two levels:

1   As a self-coaching journal for you, for your team, project or organization
2   As the fundamental coaching model for Naked Coaching

Every time you have achieved 'success', by your own definition, you have followed this formula:

> ▪
>
> Know where you want to go.
> Know where you are now.
> Know what you have to do, to get to where you want to go.
> Do it!
>
> ▪

And the first is one of the biggest challenges in life – and it is a challenge that has to be overcome, because if we do not know where we want to go, we have no chance of ever getting there.

What's your dream? – and only think the *what*, not the how – that will come later.

Strategy One: Continuous Writing

Starting on the next page, write down your biggest dream, your great-est ambition, with one powerful difference: *the pen or pencil must not leave the paper, at any time.*

Approach this with an open mind. Start writing, and only stop when you want to stop. It may seem strange at first, no 'i's will be dotted, no 't's crossed, as your pen will not leave the paper, until you have finished. At the end of each line, your pen will go to the start of the next line with a pen or pencil line.

Do this for about ten lines and something very special will hap-pen – those dreams that lie deep within you will come to the surface. Your conscious mind will, in effect, give over to your sub-conscious mind. And you will find yourself writing *automatically*. Keep going – if you can write for two pages. You may discover something about yourself that you did not know at a conscious level.

My Dream:

Outcomes/Exact Results

You now have your dream or an idea of your dream. Now, ask yourself, what will the exact results be when you have achieved your dream?

Be as clear and certain as you can – there is no room for ambiguity here. If it is promotion, write down the new job title and your new responsibilities. If your dream is 'to be rich' write down how much you will have in your account, by when.

My outcomes:

By when:

Journey Two – Self-Coaching – Applying The Formula to You

KNOW WHERE YOU ARE NOW

Are you in ownership of your life?
(Write down Yes or No here):

Do you take complete accountability and responsibility for everything and anything that ever happens to you? If you do, great – you know where you are right now in this massive wonder we call life. If not, great – as long as you accept that not knowing is a choice you are making.

Taking true and total, personal ownership is one of the most powerful things we can ever do. The main reason we sometimes do not do this is because we seek the approval of others. Write down here whose approval you need in life:

OK – go get their approval.

Deep down, you already know this stuff; because this stuff is what you have been doing all of your life, in all areas of your life, whenever and wherever you achieve 'success' by your own definition. So, if you already know it, why do you not do it? What is stopping you?

Fear – a four letter word.

You have to address and overcome that four letter word, before you can move on. A main reason people do not take true and total ownership is because they are in fear of some kind, often of 'failure', sometimes of 'success'.

Know this: 'Failure' is a seven letter word that is also a noun, so we can give it whatever meaning we choose – give it a meaning that gives you control over it and any hold it *has* over you, will become *had* over you.

Do this

Live a parallel life

Next Monday and Tuesday, really go for it. Be your true self and unleash your true and total personality on the world. Take action, enjoy life to the full, see the very best in everything and everybody, and help others to do the same. Surround yourself with positive people (this will happen automatically, because when other people can do something themselves, or believe they can, they want to tell you that you can too). Smile when you see the sun, laugh when you feel happy, bubble with love, energy and the thrill of being alive.

On Wednesday and Thursday, go for nothing. Be that impostor who inhabits your thoughts and body, do nothing, complain a lot and say that life has got it in for you, bring others down by telling them how you feel. Surround yourself with negative people (this will happen automatically, because when other people can't do something themselves, or believe they can't, they want to tell you that you can't either). Frown when you see the sun, cry when you feel sad, freeze with fear and the nightmare of existence.

Then on Friday ask yourself this single question – which of these two days did I enjoy more?

If it was Monday and Tuesday – live like that every day.

If it was Wednesday and Thursday – live like that every day.

▪

Worry

Select a Worry Hour. Have an hour of the week when you always worry – and do not worry at any other time. Sundays at 4 p.m. is a great time to worry, as is Thursday at 8 a.m. If you find yourself having any thoughts that do not serve you, at any other time, simply delay them until the Worry Hour.

▪

Be your own best friend. You will achieve 'wellness' in only one way, by being your own best friend.

I have always thought that the worst place to go when you are feeling ill is to the Doctor's, everyone just sitting around spreading and receiving bugs! In our world today, much of the health agenda is around physical and mental cure, and physical prevention. The purpose here is to open up our minds simply to this possibility – that within us, right now, we have the capacity to radically improve our *wellbeing*. There are many physical things that we can do, such as breathing properly, relaxation and meditation. All good stuff. And the most powerful way is, simply, to be *your own best friend*. By loving yourself, unconditionally. Loving everything that you are – your gifts, your talents, your personality, your 'faults'.

Now, of course, there may be certain negative phrases that rush into your mind right now:

- ▪ How arrogant is that?
- ▪ That's very big headed, David.
- ▪ How selfish!

I don't mean by arrogantly shouting from the rooftops 'Hey look at me, I'm fantastic' – we only do that when we need others to tell us we are great. I don't mean by being defensive when someone, anyone, 'attacks' us with something they say, or do – we only do that when we need to prove that they are 'wrong' and we are 'right'. I mean by simply admitting to ourselves what we already know, and what we have always known: that we are unique, amazing and wonderful. And by *showing* others this, each and every day, by your actions, by who you are.

To simply love yourself, without condition, always. And to encourage others to do the same, by believing in others' unique gifts – even total strangers ...

■

I was on a radio phone-in. A man phoned in and said:

'Hi David. I've been sat here listening to you going on and on about success. Well let me tell you this. I have never achieved anything in my life. I can't read or write. I'm one of the forgotten few. What do you say to me then?'

On live radio – cue heartbeat and perspiration!

I talked about choices being available to us all, how it is never too late to learn to read or write and even if he did not do this, because interpersonal skills are more important these days, there were still plenty of dreams he could make happen. He was having none of it.

'What you don't realize, David, is that it's all very well for you sitting in your comfy studio, spouting off about this and that – what about people like me who have no hope, none?'

Part of me wanted to share my personal struggles and times of hardship. I didn't; I changed tack.

'OK, tell me, what would you like to achieve in your life? I know you don't think you ever will, but please, tell me just one thing you would like to do'. After a pause, he softened and said, 'I'd love to be a car mechanic.'

'Great,' I said.

I spoke too soon ... because he then said: 'And I don't know anything about cars.'

Then I said the word. I don't know where it came from, that didn't matter. I leaned slightly closer towards the microphone and simply said 'Yet'.

He said: 'What?'

And I repeated it, saying: 'You don't know anything about cars, *yet*'.

To which he simply said: 'Thank you,' and rang off.

That was a year ago. Just a few days before I wrote this, I received a card in the post. It was a single business card, inside a Thank You card. Nothing was written on the card – there was no need for that. Because the card was a business card for this man, who is now a successful car mechanic.

I called him straight away to say well done. He apologized for not writing anything in the card, saying to me: 'I know a lot about cars, and they know a lot about me. And I couldn't put anything on the card, because I haven't learned to read or write. Yet.'

■

'Yet' is a magic word, because it does not question whether your dreams will happen, and come true. Indeed, it doesn't even ask you when. It simply reinforces that it, or they, will happen. They just haven't happened yet.

And some. Because the word rekindles our dreams, and hopes, and bypasses our fears about whether we are up to going for them, it automatically brings them closer – uppermost in our mind, more real in our hearts, tingling in our selves. And so they seem easier, more achievable, and inspire us into taking action, now, or very, very soon.

So next time you think about what you want, take ownership; and when you decide to make a true decision – that's when *you* decide you are ready – just close your eyes, think about, see, and touch your dream, and say to yourself that one word 'Yet.'

And feel what you feel. Trust me, when you open your eyes, you will have made that decision. And to help others, all you have to do, is simply love yourself, then you will love others, every day.

Simply? Simply!

Please, read and re-read the next paragraph, and remember it forever.

■

If you are not your own best friend, and do not love yourself, no-one else will, because you won't let them. And you will be unable to love another, and put other people first. Because you will be unsure of your own worth, you will keep stealing from others. When you love yourself, you have no need to do this, because you know that you are more than enough. Besides, this is not a dress rehearsal; you cannot rehearse being you. You are you, and you, those whose lives that you touch, your communities and organizations, and your world, need you to do this, for them.

■

In life, we – all of us who have not achieved self-actualization (please remember I am travelling on this journey with you) – look for compliments from others, and sometimes score 'points' from others by running them down, making ourselves feel superior to others by 'taking' from them. This is the ego life.

As you are reading this, you may be remembering all that we learned at school that we could not do. Just look at the rules that were set in our schools. Picture your teacher standing in front of your class:

1　'I am the teacher, you are the children, I therefore know the answers and you are here to learn them.'
2　'I will teach you in small pieces, ready for you to discover the big picture after you have left us – in your own time.'
3　'Everything you will learn here will be theory; it will not help you in any way in your life, or your career.'
4　'While you are learning, you will not talk, unless I ask you a question or you put your hand in the air, and only then if I give you permission.'
5　'You will not walk around – except between lessons, when you will need to be an Olympic athlete, reaching your next class in a matter of minutes.'
6　*'You will never, ever cheat.'*

To love yourself, you must reverse these rules – the more you reverse, the more the love grows. Say to yourself, now:

1　I know a great deal about life, and I learn new things every day. However, I do not *have to* 'learn' anything that I do not choose in order to be successful, unless I choose to do so, because my definition of success is entirely up to me. And by the way, I'm pretty amazing.
2　I am the big picture, because I am alive and in this world. I can't hang around to find out if there is a bigger picture because my

time is limited, and I have much to do, and I need to get started now.

3   Unless the film *The Matrix* turns out to be true and we are not real, then I am as real as they come. I feel pain in life, and that is real, and so I will go out and seek pleasure as well, as is my birthright. And by the way, I create my own 'reality'.

4   I have many questions and, while I learn and help others, I will communicate whenever and however I choose, as long as I am not hurting or upsetting anyone else. I love to listen, and to pay total and absolute attention to other people, and to the reality around me. And because I am free to speak my mind, I choose to listen even more.

5   When I am learning, experiencing and living, I need to experience and meet different people. This is a fantastic time to be alive: I can go into cities and meet people from all over the world – travelling has never been easier – and hey, I can play chess with anyone else in the world that I choose.

6   I cheat with pride – as long as it is not breaking the law or hurting another human being. If someone else has discovered something I have not, hey, I want the details, and I will do what they have done.

When you become your own best friend, and truly love yourself, you reclaim your birthright, and you are free to look at leadership from a different perspective – your own. You no longer 'judge' others by your own set of beliefs and values.

One powerful way to make this happen fast is by just thinking about what you are thinking. The power of positive thinking is well documented, and we move to higher degrees of 'wellness' when we focus on what we want, not on what we don't want.

What's starting you?

Ask yourself a different question next time you are faced with a big challenge: 'What's starting you?' Not what we so often ask ourselves: 'What's stopping you?' In heads in houses across the globe. In teams in organizations around the world. In conversation between you and me, right now.

Scene One – the assertive approach

- Me – 'What's stopping you?'
- You – 'Nothing.'
- Me – 'So why have you not done everything you want to have done, especially those one or two really big things you have in your mind, right now?'
- You – 'Anything I say will be an excuse.'
- Me – 'Of course, because there is nothing stopping you at all, so go and do something about it right now.'
- You – 'Thank you.'
- Me – 'My pleasure.'

Result? Nothing happens.

■

Scene Two – the counselling approach

- Me – 'What's stopping you?'
- You – 'Well, I've got this problem, and this thing happened to me.'
- Me – 'Would it help if you shared it with me right now?'
- You – 'Yes, I think so.'
- Me – 'In your own time.'
- You – 'Well.'
- You then talk openly about what is wrong with you, and relive over and over the circumstances, making you feel a lot, er, better?
- Me – 'Oh, we're out of time today, I think we've made good progress. We will talk more next time. Just leave your cheque with my receptionist on the way out … '

Result? We have reinforced our negative feelings by going on and on about them.

■

Scene Three – the dependence approach

- ▪ Me – 'What's stopping you?'
- ▪ You – 'Well, I can't … '
  … feel confident without alcohol.'
  … feel relaxed without tablets.'
  … be me without you.'
  … etc.

Result? You lose ownership of your life.

▪

When we ask ourselves the question 'What's stopping us?', we think about what is 'wrong' with us, and often push one of our 'self-destruct' buttons. When we ask ourselves the question 'What's starting us?', we think about what is 'right' with us, and often push one of our 'self-construct' buttons.

Now, think back to the really big decisions you have made in your life – on relationships, family, career, where you will live, what you will do. I bet your thought process went through something like this:

You analysed the pros and cons of your situation, and choices, and then, at a certain moment, and one you can remember right now, as you read this, you said to yourself: 'That's it, enough now – that is what I am going to do/who I am going to be.' And as you said that, waves of energy and excitement rushed through your entire body, your very being. And you knew that was what was going to happen, that nothing was going to stop you, because what was starting you was an unstoppable force.

And we can help others in the same way – *what's starting you?* What is fantastic about being part of this team? What is amazing about this project? You help others to be themselves, and to be their own best friend – by who you are, what you do, and by helping them to focus on their dreams, not their nightmares.

It is only once we realize this, that we can help others to do exactly the same. And by doing so, we proclaim our uniqueness, while respecting others' uniqueness as well. For, in the 21st century, the real leaders will be the people with a unique personality, skill or product.

And uniqueness never drops out of committees; it arises from deep within a person, from your essential self.

There is a second, very powerful reason to be our own best friend. If we do not do this, we can never, that's *never,* truly love another. If we do not love ourselves without condition, we will never find fulfilment with another, because fulfilment can never be found in another person, it has to already be within ourselves. Only then can you choose to be fulfilled, *with* another person.

It is the difference between being in a relationship, and the two of you making one whole, and therefore being two half people, or retaining the 'you', all of you, and also choosing together to be a third 'person'. One plus one equals three.

Society and mass market messages contrive to prevent this happening:

First, the idea that we are 'young, free and single' suggests that we are destined to be 'old, imprisoned and married'.

Second, we never have to sacrifice our *self* to be in a loving relationship – we cannot, once we love ourselves, and we love ourselves first. As we have unlimited love, and because our own need is full, we have plenty (and that is plenty) left over.

Third, we never have to *work* at our relationships. We spend enough time at work, no matter how much fun we are having. You don't have to work at your relationships when you love yourself.

Fourth, this is not selfish, indeed, quite the reverse, for when we love ourselves, all the time, we do not need to 'steal' love or affection, or points from other people.

How will you know when you are truly your own best friend, when you truly love yourself? Unconditionally? You will know, and you will:

- Help other people every day – opportunities to do this will present themselves to you, automatically, in life.
- Feel wonderful 24/7 – you will go around with a grin on your face and other people won't quite know why.
- You will lose arguments, and love to do so – especially at home with your partner/children/family.

And, in the most significant paragraph:

- Every day, you will come from a place of love, and never fear or hate. You will send out radiance, warmth and love to everyone that you meet. You will do this when you meet people in person, on the phone, by email and with every communication. And when you are in conversation, you will always talk about the other person's favourite subject – themselves.

This does not mean giving in, it does not mean you will never make mistakes or do things you later regret – it does mean that from this moment on you will never again have any fears about whether you are being liked by other people because:

- It won't matter – you love yourself, and the love you will attract from all around you will keep you overflowing for many many centuries.
- They will like you anyway, because you will be so self-certain, with such genuine care and compassion for others, always putting them first.

This is all powerful, and a pre-requisite to moving on. Please, you must love yourself. This is not a dress rehearsal we are in, and anyway, you can't rehearse being you, you can only be you.

■

Love yourself, unconditionally, and watch what happens within you, around you, and for others …

■

Because as 'wellness' applies to you, and to us, so it does to each other. It applies in every place throughout our world where and when we are with others. We have different degrees of 'wellness', as do our teams at work, our communities at home, and our world. And the same thinking applies – we move to higher degrees of 'wellness' when we focus on what we want, not on what we don't want.

Nightmares are very powerful, and so are dreams. We invent our own nightmares, and they are also invented for us by other people – by parents telling us not to talk to strangers, by discussions of risk in our organizations, by endless discussions on what can go wrong, by politicians, who frighten us to vote for them so that we can stay safe.

We will feel very alone, and often very guilty, when we lose a loved one. To remove these feelings, which your loved one would not want you to have …

Rosalind and I had the great fortune to see Ben Zander at the Oxford University Union. Ben is the conductor of The Boston Philharmonic Orchestra and he is the most inspiring presenter I have ever seen. It is in my memory as if it was yesterday. During the Zander Experience, Ben plays a piece on his piano – Chopin's E Minor Prelude. The choice of music does not matter – how we listen does. So, please, select a favourite classical or other relaxing track, and follow through the Ben story, now, as you listen …

Ben started to play, and as he did, he shared with us what we may be thinking …

'Sounds OK.'

'I wonder how long it is.'

'What shopping do we need for the weekend?'

'When does this thing finish?'

Ben then asked everyone to close their eyes and bring to mind someone dear to us who had recently passed away. Someone whom we missed. Really missed …

Now, please, play the music you have selected again. This time, do the above – from start to finish, eyes closed, with every thought and emotion focused on your loved one no longer with you …

On a Wednesday afternoon in May 2004, I was present when wonder came alive. With tears rolling down my cheeks, I was touched by an overwhelming loss, and deep, deep sadness, and through all of these feelings, I found closure, and joy, and inner peace.

We can all experience closure – drawing a line on a bad experience and placing it in the past, on a memory without feeling bad, or closing a loved one lost, without forgetting them – indeed, their love inside of us seems stronger than ever.

www.benjaminzander.com

Deep peace of the running wave to you.
Deep peace of the flowing air to you.
Deep peace of the quiet earth to you.
Deep peace of the gentle night to you.
Deep peace of the infinite peace to you.

Gaelic Blessing

DO NOT READ THIS PAGE unless there is something still holding you back:

Right now, you, and every single person you can be, and every single person that you know, and every single person reading this book, have one thing in common. You are all going to die – you, that's right, you.

One day, you will close your eyes, stop breathing and die.
So, why would you fear anything?

My father died at Wexford Hospital in September 1983. He had survived three previous heart attacks and always amazed people with his positive attitude. This time it was different – he was subdued and quiet, and one talk with the doctor confirmed my biggest fear: he was not going to make it.

I was sitting with him, when he suddenly opened his eyes. He looked at me and smiled. That smile sent a warmth through me that I still feel today. Then he said he had to tell me something, that it was important because he would not make it through the night as he'd had enough and didn't want to fight any more.

That's when he said it.

'Tim, this is not a dress rehearsal!'

'Sorry?'

'Life needs to be lived because, I promise you, this is it.'

'Yes, Dad, I know.'

'Looking at how you live your life, I don't think you do. Promise me you'll think about what I'm saying and DO something about it.'

'Yes, Dad, I promise.'

Then he gripped my hand very hard and said:

'Remember. Then I can die happy – your life is not a dress rehearsal.'

Those were the last words he ever shared with me. My dad died next to me, as I held his hand, just after midnight on Monday 19 September, 1983, the same moment in which I decided to start living as if I meant it.

Tim Drohan

▪

The moment in your life when you had your whole life in front of you …

When we look at newborn babies we often say to ourselves, or out loud, 'Isn't it wonderful, they have their whole life ahead of them.'

Check you have a pulse. Go on, feel the beat of your pulse right now. If you can, rejoice, you are alive. And you have the whole of your life in front of you. Whoever you are, wherever you are, and whatever your age. Right now.

Perhaps you think about yourself as 'middle-aged'. How do you know? We have no idea whatsoever when the 'middle' is happening. *Out of 130 million babies born each year worldwide, four million survive for less than four weeks.* So, for two million people each year, their *middle-age* was fourteen days old.

There is only one thing certain about your life, and that is your death and departure from this world. Of course you know this with your left brain; you may have completed your will, taken out your life insurance, planned ahead.

Please read the story of what happened to the Hanson family below and, as you do, think about that one action, that one idea, that one thing that you have been meaning to do or say for a long time – and do it now, today.

▪

Christine Hanson, 3, from Massachusetts was travelling with her parents, Peter Hanson and Sue Kim Hanson, to California on Flight 175, which was flown into the World Trade Centre on September 11, 2001.

Peter Hanson, 32, was a software company vice-president with the presence of mind to phone his parents from the doomed aircraft.

Sue Kim Hanson, 35, was a medical student working on a doctoral thesis that promised to reveal the workings of a chemical believed to regulate immune responses.

Christine Hanson, 3, was on her first trip to Disneyland.

■

What magic will you leave behind?

I happened to be in Salzburg recently, in the same week as Mozart's 250th birthday. I wondered how big the celebrations would be – my wonder was answered as we came in to land: 'Welcome to Amadeus airport, in the year of Wolfgang Amadeus Mozart's birth, during which we are holding 250 major events to celebrate the magic he brought to our lives.'

And then a feeling of great sadness flooded through me – it is a feeling I have had about Mozart before, and this time it was deeper. What an amazing talent, perhaps the greatest composer that ever lived, dying so young, so poor, and with so few friends.

You and I may not die penniless; we may live longer, and have more friends, so when we do leave this earth, what magic will we be remembered for?

■

Your living obituary/eulogy

Write your own obituary, as you would like it to appear in a newspaper, or write what you would like to be said about you at your funeral – you will be writing in the third person.

■

In your life, I am sure you will have been told things like:

'You are good.'

'You are bad.'

'You are clever.'

'You are stupid.'

When, of course, the greatest miracle that we can ever know is:

'You are.'

'You are.'

Think of all the expressions we have invented that suggest we cannot be more than we have become:

'Keep your feet on the ground.'

'Get real.'

'Don't get ideas above your station.'

'Get your head out of the clouds.'

'You are not the finished article.'

Theodore Roosevelt said: 'Keep your feet on the ground, and your eyes on the stars.'

As you know, 'reality' or 'facts' are not as they are, they are as you are. Indeed, 'Don't get ideas above your station' because your station/ambition/dreams are so massive, it would not be possible to do so. 'Get your head out of the clouds' must be some kind of hang-gliding term. And finally, no, 'You are not the finished article'. That will only happen when you are in your coffin.

That doesn't stop our inner voice from sometimes telling us otherwise. You know the one – the one that chatters on and on, endlessly, telling us what we can and cannot do, what we have done wrong in the past, on and on and on.

If you are asking yourself, right now: 'What's this inner voice then?'– *that's the one!*

Some call this our ego. Our ego has convinced us that the golden key of enlightenment simply doesn't exist. Indeed, anyone who claims they have found it is wrong. Anyone still looking for it is on a hopeless quest. Of course these people are not making an 'excuse' about their own happiness and wellbeing, because as the key to such things does not exist, they can never find it, and it's not their fault. It's just this thing called 'life'. And the lengths these people will go to, to convince themselves that it does not exist, are unlimited …

The most frequent phrase I hear on leadership courses is: 'I am probably the most cynical person in this group,' or similar. This establishes their belief systems and their superiority over the rest of the group, who have mistakenly come along to the event to learn or have new choices. They then go on to argue with the material, arguing that it can't work because of this, that, or the other.

If you consider yourself to be a cynic, don't read on, it will be too uncomfortable for you.

For a change: oh dear, you read on anyway …

Most people are seeking the golden key that will unlock their lives and set them on the road to their dreams. Deep inside, they hope that this key exists. Hoping such a key exists, they keep looking. However, they are also aware that finding the key may bring new fears and challenges, so they go out of their way to argue that such a key does not exist. By convincing themselves that it does not exist, they will naturally never find it – and then neither will anyone. And that's not their fault.

Those that look within, and stop seeking, find it.

The golden key lies within you. You have greater skills than you may have ever dreamed possible – so use these to make a decision, and take that first action. And if that action doesn't work, do something else, and if that doesn't work, do something else ... and if you are cynical about this, then you are cynical about yourself.

Of all the things you believe in, you do not include yourself.

Where you are is far more comfortable than the possibility that you can be so much more in a matter of a heartbeat – that moment you make a different choice.

Three questions:

▪ Has anyone else, with the exact same circumstances as you, made their dreams come true?
▪ What is the worst thing, the single biggest event, that could go wrong by you making that decision, reconnecting with that person, or ... ?
▪ Has anyone else with less of a financial start in life than you had, or have now, gone on to make a fortune?

On money, on achieving peace, on anything: the easiest option in the world is to say it is not possible. It is easy to be cynical; it is far, far more rewarding to take action.

And being cynical is a choice that you are making. It is your ego that tells you this is the only choice to make, and it is not. Many others are making different choices. Your ego would call these people 'optimists' – that is only half their story. They would rather be an 'optimist', and wrong, than a 'pessimist', and right.

And, by the way, if breathing is important to you, optimists live longer.

Your ego asks all of the incessant questions, of yourself, and of the world. And so ... the second stage of achieving total peace is to quieten our ego. Imagine right now, that I was to put on a wizard's suit, produce a magic wand and offer you three wishes ... one for each of you. For you are three different people, in one body.

Firstly, there is the you that you show to the world, the you that you want others to see. That is your Public You. Some call this your ego. This is where your inner voice resides, when it talks to you, logically, and never shuts up chattering.

Then there is the you that is full of fear, of worries, of uncertainties. That is the Fearful You. The part of you that is always telling you that you are not liked, not good enough or have something missing. This is also where your inner voice resides, when it shouts at you, loudly, and *even louder* when you tell it to shut up.

Finally there is the you that knows how amazing you are – the real, authentic, True You. This you is absolutely certain about who you are; it comes from love in everything it does, and it finds value in everyone. This is where your true, authentic voice resides, where it whispers to you, warmly, whenever you choose to listen.

And to make it even more confusing, we change between the three many times, each and every day.

Now, how can you move your first two 'selves' aside, so that you will never feel fear, doubt and worry again?'

■

Imagine I was a magician, complete with magic wand, and I offered you three wishes, one for each of your three 'selves' – your ego, your fearful and your true.

Your ego's wish would be something like 'I wish to be popular'. And with a single stroke of my wand it would be true.

■

Your ego asks constantly for something that has already happened. People do like you, and your ego needs this to be reinforced, each and every day. Indeed, your ego gives you an appetite for being popular that is not only insatiable; it can never, ever be satisfied. Some people like you, some do not – and, I hate to hurt your ego here, other people really don't spend that much time thinking or talking about you, anyway.

■

Your fearful self, if it ever believed in wishes in the first place, would eventually pluck up the courage with 'I'd like to re-move failure from my life, forever. Please, if it is not too much trouble.' No trouble at all, and with a second stroke of my wand it would be true.

■

Your fearful self asked to remove something that it makes up itself. Failure, like all nouns, only has the meaning that you choose to give it. You are the one that is giving it a meaning that is not helping you, so you are the one who can give it another meaning at any time that you choose. One thing's for certain – you can't fight it. Whoever heard of declaring war on a noun? So, you can love it, or you can make it disappear.

▪

Now your third wish – what would your real, authentic voice like?

▪

First we have to remove the first two voices, not shut them up, just quieten them. To do this, acknowledge them, thank them and feel them floating up inside your mind, till they disappear. And as this happens, please read this one word, and do whatever it says:

▪

STOP

▪

Just STOP

Just stop. Right now, stop reading, stop thinking, stop analysing. Wherever you are right now, just close your eyes, put the book down for a while, and simply stop … Really, please, put the book down and return later – stop now.

▪

STOP

▪

And as you did this, a very powerful thing happened … with a quiet, warm and wonderful knowing, your true, authentic voice appeared, and this true voice whispers: *'I need nothing, I have everything, I am.'*

And you felt the stirring of something deep in your heart, some-thing very warm and special. Something so wonderful and amazing that no words in the English language can describe them. You know that feeling when you first fell in love, and that excitement you had when you woke up as a child on Christmas morning, and all of the moments in your life when you felt like yelling out 'Wow' all together, combined, in one, single magical feeling. And with no stroke of the wand whatsoever, your wish comes true, without you even making it. For the loving you only has one wish.

To be present.

Peace. Absolute total peace. No noise, no music, not a sound. And then from somewhere deep within, in your head and your heart your love returns, and whispers: '*You are enough; you have enough, and I love you, just as you are.*' And you are found.

Sometimes, we have moments when we know that who we are is enough. When what happens to us, or around us, has no effect, or impact on how we feel. That is when the ego is quietened, not because it is satisfied, rather because it has disappeared within the greater, loving self. And it only takes such a moment. And in that moment we stop. Then we are above the rush, and time itself, and in those moments, however fleeting, we hear stillness.

Of course you will feel stressed again in the future. And this time there will be a difference – this time you will enjoy it!

Be uncomfortable. Be uncertain. Be fearful And anything else you want to. *As long as you are enjoying it.*

Don't analyse it, just smile, because we can feel 'failure', and laugh about it; we can fall in love with risk; we can find the wonder in everything and anything, and in any moment.

So, please: worry; be stressed; lose sleep. As long as, and only as long as, you are enjoying it.

Of course, ask questions in life; simply don't ask those questions that you have no need of asking of yourself. Those that take you into ever decreasing, *vicious* circles. Instead, enjoy life as it is, and how you are, and how, as you are, you can take life forward – then you will be in an ever increasing, *victorious* circle. And we can do this at any time …

You know those moments in life when you say to yourself or to another person: 'When we look back at this, we'll laugh?' Well, don't wait – laugh now. Be now. Without asking question after question, or even the same question over and over … without seeking and looking …

And you will have arrived where you always were – within. Where you have always been, where you are right now. You have come home. In fact, you have never really been away.

▪

Being lost is worth the coming home.

Neil Diamond

▪

■

On the final day, in the final session of my Leadership Master Classes, I ask everyone to write down one amazing strength/attribute/quality about themselves, and to do the same for everyone else with whom they have shared the experience.

These are written on adhesive notes, one for each person, so that on a course of ten people, each person will end up with ten separate adhesive notes, each with one inspiring and amazing comment on it, covering all ten people. They then take it in turn to stand up, share what they have written about themselves, and hear from the other nine about themselves, while they are standing at the front of the room. After each person speaks, they then stick the adhesive note onto the person. It is powerful beyond description, stays in the memory forever, and is without doubt the most powerful way to close any leadership event.

On an event in early 2004, the most amazing thing happened. Alan Hutchinson was one of the delegates, and when his turn came to share his thoughts with the first person standing, he said:

'You will be successful, because you are you.'

and stuck on the adhesive note.

I remember thinking, 'That's a bit general. Maybe he didn't get time to write anything more specific.'.

The second delegate stood up, and we went round the room again. When it came to Alan he stood up and said:

'You will be successful, because you are you.'

Now I was curious. What was he up to – here was everyone else being very personal, and Alan had said exactly the same thing, using exactly the same words, to both delegates.

Alan was seated such that in three goes, he would be standing up. Sure enough, after the next delegate – and these people had become so much more than that: they had become friends – Alan stood up and said again:

'You will be successful, because you are you.'

Now I was interested. I glanced around the room. Because I was the facilitator I was able to observe, and I saw what I always saw. Absolute focus, attention and energy in the room, on what people were saying, what others were hearing, on handshakes and hugs, and on avoiding certain parts of each other's anatomies as the adhesive notes were 'posted'.

Two to go to Alan standing up. Surely, I thought, he had not spent his entire hour's preparation for this writing out ten times on adhesive notes:

'You will be successful, because you are you.'

No, he had not. For the next two, the same: he stood up, always looking directly into their eyes, and very, very sincerely saying: 'You will be successful, because you are you.' Now it was to be his turn to stand up. With an amazing mix of wonder, anticipation, and some anxiety, I watched Alan stand up.

Surely he would not say it again.

No, he did not. He said:

'I will be successful, because I am me.'

■

That afternoon, I moved from concern to confusion to anxiety to curiosity to interest to wonder to admiration to joy and finally to me, too, arriving home. *All in 30 minutes.* And then it hit me – as I had been sharing these messages, and listening to leaders around the world, while travelling on these journeys myself, I had missed the one, key, fundamental message that sums it all up.

I had been putting together this message as a jigsaw puzzle, travelling around, finding pieces here and finding pieces there. I had often thought how exciting (and frustrating) it all was, because although I was gathering together many pieces, I had nothing to compare them to, because I had no picture on the front of the box.

And in those 30 minutes I rejoiced, because I finally realized, life is not about putting the pieces together – it is a lot more fun when they are rattling around inside. No, life is about looking at the picture on the box. For, on the front of the box, is a picture.

And, of course, that picture is of you.

■

You have no need to find yourself, because you have already done so; all you can choose to do, is return to yourself.

You are not quite sure what it is, this thing … and you don't have to be.

It is there for all of us to feel and taste and we don't have to see it.

It can climb mountains, defeat our worst fears and lift our weary heads.

It's an amazing gift, one that many search for throughout their lifetimes.

Stop searching non-believers, your journey is at an end.

The gift waits, quietly unwrapped in the centre of your body.

Just breathe deeply … be a great human being – because you are the gift and the gift is you …

Alastair Lukies

■

Journey Two – Self-Coaching –
Applying the Formula to You

KNOW WHAT YOU HAVE TO DO, TO GET TO WHERE YOU WANT TO GO

■

You know your dream and outcome.
You are in ownership of your life.
You have listed your choices of action.
And choices are at the heart of this part of the formula.
Note that I say choices, not changes.
Change is irrelevant because it is happening all the time
– it is our choices that shape our future, that decide what
happens next.

■

Deep down, you already know this, it is obvious.

Yes, knowing we have choices is obvious. What is not so obvious
is which choices will 'work'.

■

I was coaching in-company, an event called 'One Team – One
Vision'. At the start I asked the team what they most wanted to
achieve from the day. One person said: 'To get as many ideas as
possible on being one team.' He did not mean this – if he had
really wanted 'as many ideas as possible' he would have been
better off going to a search engine – I have just typed it into
Google and found over sixty million hits – 66,700,000 – more
than I could probably cover in a day, or a lifetime.

■

What he meant, and what we all mean, and why we buy books, and why we go to events, is that we are looking for 'the best ideas'. And that is only our first challenge, or excuse, for not deciding on a choice to take. The second is that it has to be the 'right' one – by our own definition. And, hey – we've already touched on this argument in Journey One, and this book isn't about arguments.

It's about action.

Just before you take that action, please allow me to give you some guidance. Given our deal, you can take it on board or not. After all, who am I to give you advice about coaching, life or leadership? I am just an ordinary guy. However, I have worked with many people, teams and companies. So, far be it for me to stop you taking that first action. However, if you will humour me a little, please open your mind to what I have found …

Advice on choices – One

You will never achieve lasting happiness by just rearranging your life.

■

Buying more goods and gadgets, moving to a new house, meeting and marrying a new partner. None of these will ever make you happy, truly and deeply happy, fulfilled and enlightened.

That doesn't stop us trying. And, of course, when we listen to that new CD, see our team score a goal, or hold the hand of the person that we love, we experience what we might call happiness. Yet it will never last for long, certainly not forever, because all of those things are external – people, events, things. We make endless lists, we change jobs, we dream, and yet so many people tell me about this inner, deep sense that there must be something more.

Time has become one of our shortest, most valuable commodities – and yet today we have the same time available to us as did our forefathers, and theirs before them. It just seems as if there is less time, because we are all so much busier, with so much more to do.

After all, previous generations never had the kind of busy lives – jobs and careers – we have today. They certainly never had fast food (except as a description of the food getting away when they were trying to catch it) or, of course, so many gadgets, tools and techniques for helping us make better use of our time, to be more in control.

We have physical diaries, time managers and calendars to ease our lives in our planning. We have email to save us time in letter writing and to speed up communications, to ease our lives in our time management, and of course to help deliver a paperless office. We have mobile devices – phones to ease our contact with each other, and more organizers than we have time to organize.

And of course, we still have 24 hours in each day – exactly the same time we have always had since we first developed a system for measuring time.

The great irony of all of the devices we have to help give us back our lives is that they do the complete opposite. We go to bed after working so hard, and yet feel there is so much undone. Never mind, tomorrow will be a new day …

And then we have so much more knowledge than we used to. Data and information is everywhere these days – wars broadcast into our homes as they happen, 24-hour news channels in every language, and the Internet giving us access to the most powerful library in the world.

■

More new information has been produced in the last 30 years than in the previous 5000. A weekday edition of the *New York Times* contains more information than average people in seventeenth-century England were likely to come across in their lifetime. The amount of information available in the world has doubled in the last five years, and it keeps doubling.

John C. Maxwell
Leadership 101: What Every Leader Needs to Know

■

Have all of these life-helping devices, and all of this information, helped us, as individuals? I believe we have not evolved; we have devolved. And of course, that is where holidays come in.

You have decided to get away from it all, and so you phone the Travel Agent.

'I want a nice long holiday please,' you say.

'Why would you like to go?'

You reply: 'Don't you mean, where would I like to go?'

'I know where you would like to go, I am asking you why?'

You think this must be some sort of promotional offer or loyalty scheme – find out what is behind our customer's intentions and earn a big bonus. You play along:

'Because I want to escape, just for a while, from my daily routine. I want to be able to relax. I want to get away.'

The Travel Agent replies: 'And how can you do this?'

You now wish you had booked online – you are losing your patience. 'Listen, I just need a holiday!'

'And what then? A week, two weeks to get away from it all, something that will cost you a fortune, is over in a flash, and all too soon all you will have are memories.'

'I assume you don't work on commission,' you say, and then ring off.

▪

Holidays, getting away from what? From all this urgency. So many of us feel that we need to reorganize things, and that if we can just do that, then things, life, will be different, better, and then we will be happy …

And the great irony of holidays is that so many of us use this valuable time to continue to reorganize our lives, and with mobile everything available, it doesn't matter where we go, we can never get away … and even if we leave those devices behind, we still have our thoughts, and so we sit on the beach, or on the train or car each day, reorganizing our thoughts and lives … until we become exhausted.

Stress, unhappiness and, at the very least, looking for more are no longer exceptions; they have become the *norm* – and there's a key word.

The Emperor's New Clothes story has popped up several times in the *Naked Leader* books, and it comes to mind once again. Perhaps we do what we do, and believe what we believe, about time, about 'busyness', about life, because it is the norm, i.e. the majority of people do it. Are you going to be the child that shouts out from the crowd? You don't have to be, you just have to be you.

Say these words to yourself, right now. Words that you already know, have always known, deep down. And as you read these ten words, and think whatever you are thinking, perhaps those feelings of rush–rush quieten down:

▪

You will never achieve lasting happiness by rearranging your life.

▪

Advice on choices – Two

No event has any meaning other than the meaning that you choose to give it, and that includes life.

The Naked Leader

▪

It is the meaning we give to events that determines what power that event has for us/over us, and we can change that meaning at any time and stage that we choose.

The Naked Leader Experience

▪

In playing card terms, think of those two as the Queen and King of Meanings, and what I am about to share with you is the Ace of Meanings – and of Trumps, because it trumps them all. When we open our minds to this, we wake up with joy each and every day, positively looking forward to anything and everything that will happen to us. And each and every day will be the best day of our life … so far, only to be overtaken by the next.

Intrigued? Great, but it's not enough. I want you to be positively salivating.

Imagine if we did not have to give events a meaning, and also imagine if we did not ever have to look at events that happen to us, wondering which meaning serves us best – in short, imagine if we could switch the definition of every event from being *one we choose*, to *one that chooses us*.

OK – simply decide that every single thing that ever happens to us, within us, and around us, happens for only one reason: to help bring our dreams closer.

■

Every single thing that ever happens to us, within us, and around us, happens for only one reason – to help bring our dreams closer.

■

And so, instead of waking up in the morning and asking ourselves: 'I wonder what will happen to me today (what helpful or unhelpful things will occur)?' or even: 'I wonder what will happen today to help me answer the question, what's it all about?', we say to ourselves:

'Today, anything and everything I see, hear, touch, feel and experience is confirmation that I am on the right track in life, and is evidence that life is conspiring to help my dreams come true. In fact, today will be the single best day of my life, so far.'

Puts a new fizz into the expression 'looking forward', doesn't it?

And we can use this in our private lives, with our relationships, with our organizations and with our world. Many will tell you that this is a hard thing to do. This is only because they have chosen it to be hard, because it is so different from our usual approach to such things, and because it is so totally different.

When you come from integrity, from a place of absolute love, and with total respect for yourself and for others, you deserve to find meaning. Well, now you can. And from a global perspective, now we must.

And then we apply it to life, as such: every event that ever happens to us confirms that our dreams, for ourselves, each other and this world, are moving closer – and that includes life. I now have a definition for the meaning of life, and it is supported each and every day.

I am now going to write the five simple words that sum this idea up – when you read them your reaction will prove them to be true. True, in every moment of your life, from your moment of birth to this very moment now.

We make it all up

We make it all up, this thing called life. Everything around us is make-believe, because everything around us is made up by people on the basis of their beliefs.

■

> Out of all the occurrences going on in the environment, a person selects those that have some significance for him from his own egocentric position in the total matrix.
>
> Take a football game; it is actually many different games. Each version of the events that transpired was just as 'real' to a particular person as other versions were to other people. There is no such 'thing' as a 'game' existing 'out there' in its own right, which people merely 'observe'. The game 'exists' for a person and is experienced by him only insofar as certain happenings have significance in terms of his purpose.
>
> *Albert Hastorf and Hadley Cantril*
> *– They Saw a Game: A Case Study*
> Journal of Abnormal and Social Psychology, 1954

■

And our 'realities' change over the years:

■

> My wife attended a medical training session a few years ago that had two different taped accounts of a story, and of course they were very different accounts. And the surprise came when the researcher indicated that it was the *same story* told by the *same person* 10 years apart. Time and subsequent events shape what is remembered and emphasized.
>
> *Michael Gilbert*

■

In many ways, our reason for existence is to give reason to our existence. We make it all up, so we may as well make up something that serves us.

This is the possibility, the chance, the perhaps, that life conspires, in every moment, to actively help us make our dreams come true. When we open up our minds to this possibility, we see it happen, we feel it happen. Synchronicities, meaningful coincidences, happen every day.

If you believe this, it will happen, and you will move into a virtuous circle of fun, experience and happiness. If you do not, it will not happen, and you will stay in a vicious circle of analysis, doubt and fear. And if you are thinking that this is all about brainwashing, you are absolutely right – it is just that.

When we stay as we are, in our vicious circle, we are being brainwashed by the norm.

When we choose to be more, in whatever 'more' may mean to us, we become free and liberated.

It is your choice:

■

Every single thing that ever happens to us, within us, and around us, happens for only one reason – to help bring our dreams closer.

■

Please, reflect, share this idea with someone whose life you touch, and when you are ready ...

Act 'as if' the change we seek to happen, has already been made

This works because of the way we *are* as human beings, and my discoveries on this support the 'be the very best that you already are' ethos, because 'as if' is based not on how we may be, or can aspire to be, but rather on how we already are as human beings.

Three basic premises add up to 'as if':

1 We automatically move in the direction of our most dominant thoughts

What we think about, we are. Our minds automatically move in the direction of our most dominant thoughts. What we think about, we become.

■

To see this work, ask someone to hold the thumb and first finger of each hand very close together – with a gap of about 2 mm, or $\frac{1}{10}$ of an inch. Go up to them and, with your hand and, without hurting them, open the gap by pulling their thumb and finger apart. You will be able to do this easily.

Now, look the person in the eyes and ask them if they like butterflies. If they say 'Yes', great. If they say 'No', say: 'Don't be ridiculous. Everyone likes butterflies!' Next, ask them to imagine what you are saying is true, and to go along with everything you say. Check this is OK and that they will do this.

Ask them to repeat the bringing close together of their thumb and finger. However, this time, they are holding an injured butterfly. Ask them to look at the butterfly closely. The butterfly's life is in their hands. If they can carry it to the other side of their garden, it has a good chance of living. If they let go of it, it will die for certain. Make sure they are looking at the butterfly all the time and keep repeating the messages of them saving the butterfly's life.

Now tell them that no power on earth will stop them on their mission – and therefore nothing can separate their thumb and finger, because if this were to happen the butterfly would die. Emphasize this until you are sure they have the message – you will be able to tell by their focus; is it absolutely on the 'butterfly'?

If so, and while repeating your message, again try to separate their thumb and finger. You will find it almost impossible.

This is not to prove the power we have in our fingers; rather the power we have in our focus.

▪

2   When we believe something to be true, we see the world in that way

Some people believe that there is no such thing as an original idea – that all new ideas have been 'invented' and that anything that claims to be a new idea is just a rehashed, existing one. Are you one of those people?

Other people believe there is such a thing as an original idea – that new ideas are waiting to be discovered. Are you one of those people?

You are in one group or the other – you can't be in both!

Conversation between Graham Bridgeman and David Taylor, after two columns published …

- ▪ Graham: 'We are running a sweepstake in Bristol on how long it will be before you run out of original ideas.'
- ▪ David: 'Don't worry about that, I've got plenty of original ideas left in me yet.'
- ▪ Graham: 'It's already been won.'

OK. If you are in the first group, have you ever had a new idea? The answer is clearly 'No'. And, if you are in the second group, have you ever had a new idea? The answer is clearly 'Yes'.

Because when you believe something to be true, you see the world in that way.

I worked with the board of eight from a large company, and asked them to think of as many practical uses (usual and unusual) for a small, standard paperclip as they could, in 30 minutes. They had 86 different ideas, and I was impressed.

That same afternoon I visited a school (defined as a 'sink' school – very inspiring!). I spoke with a class of eight 'problem students' and asked them to do the same, also in 30 minutes. How many did they come up with?

314.

I told them that they were 'really thinking outside of the box' to which they replied: 'What box?' For too many adults, true innovation involves thinking outside of a box that we ourselves invented! In your organization, don't think outside of the box; escape from it. Smash it to pieces, then burn it.

And guess what? The board spent half their time disagreeing with each other's suggestions. The students didn't and as a result they were the only group to come up with snow shoes for grasshoppers, performing do-it-yourself keyhole surgery, and placing it on a thin piece of wood, wiggling a magnet underneath and watching it boogie.

Oh yes, they also came up with one the board missed completely – to hold papers together.

We interpret events to support what we believe. Our sub-conscious's role in life is to support whatever our conscious mind is thinking. The challenge this gives us as human beings is that our conscious mind is the sceptical, questioning filter that we need to survive.

However, our all-powerful sub-conscious is blocked by what the conscious mind 'chooses' (i.e. what we choose) to believe to be true. Not blocked for long though …

3   Our minds cannot tell the difference between something that happens in 'reality' and something we imagine with emotional intensity

Two powerful ways to illustrate this:

■

The power of imagination

Stand up, raise your right or left arm to your side, and move it backwards, to behind your body, twisting your waist as you do so. Move your arm as far as you can, and see how far around your body it goes.

Now, with your arms by your side, close your eyes, and imagine you are repeating the same movement. This time, in your mind, 'see' your arm reach the point it reached before, and then, *easily, effortlessly and automatically* 'see' it going an-other six, maybe nine, maybe twelve inches. Maybe it goes an extra foot and a half.

Open your eyes and repeat it for real, and feel that arm stretch further than it did before.

■

And:

■

The pendulum

Whenever your mind focuses exclusively on a single thought or idea, your body responds. Dr H. Bernheim called this an 'ideomotor response'.

To do this, you will need a 'pendulum' – a piece of string with a heavy object at the base is fine.

Now:

1 Hold pendulum between thumb and forefinger.
2 Keep your hand still. Feel it getting still.
3 Close your eyes (read through these instructions first!).

In your mind, think of the pendulum swinging back and forth. Picture it, visualize it, but you are only thinking it in your mind.

- In your mind – as a picture.
- Backwards and forwards.
- Back and forth.
- While keeping your hand completely still.

Do this in your mind only for about a minute, and then open your eyes. Your pendulum will be swinging from side to side (it doesn't matter how large the swing, although the larger the swing the bigger your thought and mental picture).

The key here is that your mind wanted to respond, and to help you. The effect is caused by involuntary muscle movements of the hand induced by the operator's own mental processes. That means that a thought or idea will cause tiny micro-muscular movements to occur. This is picked up and amplified by the pendulum (or dowsing stick or any other device you happen to be using) to produce this astonishing effect.

▪

Journey Two – Self-Coaching – Applying The Formula to You

DO IT!

Go and do it – don't write it down, don't record it, don't talk about it – go and

> DO IT.
> Don't keep reading – do it!
> Ok – you keep reading, I keep ramping up the reasons.

Think of your less dominant hand (if you are right-handed it will be your left, and vice versa). Look at the little finger of your less dominant hand. What purpose does it serve you? Very little.

Now, write down all of the worries that you would exchange for losing this tiny, useless and irrelevant little finger. If you lost your finger, you would no longer worry about:

Do it!

Go and do it – don't write it down, don't record it, don't talk about it – go and DO IT.
Don't keep reading – do it!
OK – you keep reading, I keep ramping up the reasons.

▪

On rejection

Rejection has a false power over us, because it does not exist at a logical level.

When I am speaking, I sometimes (in open conference!) ask a female member of the audience if they will have dinner with me that evening. Invariably they say: 'No, thank you'. Sometimes a little too quickly!

Let's say her name is Samantha. I then say: 'Now, how am I doing?' Some people would say I have been rejected or knocked back or another inspiring thought. I don't see it like that. Was I having dinner with Samantha before I asked her? No. Am I now having dinner with Samantha? No. So, I am exactly where I was a few minutes ago.

This definition of rejection can cause great disquiet – summarized by these next two comments, frequently made/asked:

1   'No, she has destroyed your hope.'
    Destroyed my hope after one attempt! Go back to page 33 and read every line. If your 'hope' is destroyed after one attempt, it is destroyed by yourself, and you will achieve little in your life. And/or:
2   'What if she had said: "Yes"?'
    Brilliant – like saying: 'I'm going to completely disprove what you say about rejection, David, by suggesting the possibility that you won't be rejected!' Like saying, 'What I say about achieving dreams may not be true because you might actually achieve them.'
    For anyone in life:
    'Some will, some won't, so what?'

■

Dance with me lady

Many years ago, I saw a photograph in *Playboy* of a young dancer from Vancouver who was the embodiment of beauty and grace. A few months later, she was the centrefold. As a young romantic amateur composer and pianist, I placed the magazine on my piano and proceeded to write her a song called *Dance With Me Lady*. I recorded the song and took the tape to *Playboy*'s Los Angeles offices, where the Playmate liaison agreed to send it on to her.

Several weeks later, I received a lovely note from her saying that the package had arrived on her birthday and how much she liked the song. I wrote back and discovered she was in a relationship, which ended my fantasy. But I followed through on my wish to connect with her and, even though it didn't work out, it exercised my 'going for it' muscle which has served me well many times and in many ways ever since. Most recently, I called 200 visionaries, many of whom I did not know, to interview them for a documentary I am making. About 98% said yes. My lesson: even if we think there is little chance for something to happen, we never know unless we try.

Jeff Hutner, Co-founder
www.newparadigmworld.com
POB 1381
Ojai, CA 93024

■

We've talked about death before. Now, let's talk about death again.

Yours.

Forgive me raising the subject of a world without your presence in your lifetime, but this taboo subject has to be faced, especially in the context of leadership, success and helping leave the world a better place than we found it.

And another reason. I want one thing more than anything else from you as you read this – I want you to take action, and so I will do anything I can to stack up the persuasion, the pressure, the encouragement, to ensure you do just that. Not to make you do it – I cannot make you do anything, and neither can anyone else – but rather to strongly convince you that it is worth your while to do something.

The first good thing about dying is that everyone will speak very highly of you, and loads of people will attend your funeral and say even more amazingly nice things about you.

Uncomfortable though it may be, please, visit a crematorium, or a graveyard, and think about what it will feel like to be dead. No matter what your religion, I am sure you agree it will be the end of this life. Indeed, every religion encourages us to give our best in this life. Have you truly given your *best*, and helped others to do the same?

So, if you have not taken that action yet – and you want to write some stuff down, OK. This is your book, and your life, not mine.

■

Twenty years from now, you will be more disappointed by the things that you didn't do than by those that you did. So throw off the bowlines. Sail away from the safe harbour. Catch the trade winds in your sails. Explore. Dream. Discover.

Mark Twain

■

Are you ready to die?

If you were to die in one minute's time (check the clock), would you die in peace?

The answer is Yes or No.

▪

Achieving life is not the equivalent of avoiding death.

Ayn Rand

▪

If the answer is 'Yes', then you are at peace. If the answer is 'No', then what are you going to do about it, right now?

Because when that moment arrives, you will experience a sudden rush of what you had wished to do, or be. You will wonder what your legacy will be – and how you will be remembered by the world.

It will not be eyesight – like the first light you saw when you opened your eyes as a baby. It will not be insight – like the sudden inspirations you had when you were in your prime, many of which you did nothing with. It will be a sudden rush of hindsight.

What a wonderful thing hindsight is.

Look back on your life, right now, while you have the chance and choice to do so. Look back to that newborn baby that was you. What would you like to say to that child? Why not say it now, and to the next generation in general, and to your surviving loved ones, and to the world?

And now, please carry out the ultimate hindsight – in advance of it happening. Close your eyes and think back on your life, *as if* you have lived the life you were born to live, *as if* you have achieved all that you set out to, *as if* you were in peace in every moment. *As if* that golden key from within has unlocked the real, true and authentic you.

Now, open your eyes, and do it!

Journey Three

– Your Coaching Relationships

Journey Three – Your Coaching Relationships –

FINDING A COACH FOR YOURSELF

Note: One and Two in this Journey are complementary. If you read one, please read both. I suppose I could have cut and pasted the same material, and reversed the personal tenses …

Life was dull working in a shoe shop after leaving college, with little money, no weekends, and an unclear vision of the future. So I decided upon a junior role at a bank, where I met Emma, who soon became my role model. She had an amazing outlook, and was always inspiring those around her in a way I had always wanted to.

Emma taught me three invaluable lessons:
- Be on interview every day of your life;
- Believe in yourself and success is achievable; and
- You are what you choose to be.

Six years on, I am now an Area Retail Manager for the same bank leading nine outlets, having inspired others with these lessons, achieved amazing accomplishments with people who never believed they could, and through this, I too found the power of the positive. Emma never coached answers; she just gave me the skills to figure them out for myself.

Laura Pescott

1   Why might you choose to be coached?

- To help you be more successful, by your own definition.
- To gain the opportunity to share and discuss things you normally keep in your head, in total confidence.
- To raise issues that you may not be able to within your team, or at home.
- To make your business more sustainable.
- To speed up – you may not be moving forward as fast as you would wish through self-coaching.
- To benefit from another person's guidance, advice and perspective.
- To help with career decisions.
- Fundamentally, to live a more fulfilling life.

2   Where would you find a business coach?

Where would you *not* find one? They are all around you, and they are coaching you all the time.

The first question to answer is: 'Do you want one from inside your organization, or externally?' If the issues you want to raise are about internal transformation, internal coaches are great. If the issues are more personal to you, or you seek an external perspective, go for an external coach.

The most reliable way to find the right coach for you is through personal recommendation, perception and networking.

3   What are the qualities of the right business coach for me?

As you read these, you will know the questions to ask potential coaches:

■ *Experience – have they been there and done it, and made mistakes?*

And I mean, been there and done it – they must be practitioners, first and foremost, not academic scholars (unless they have then worked in real organizations with real people), and not gurus (same unless).

Question to them: Tell me the biggest business mistake you have ever made. If they have never made one, or give you a standard glib answer, do not have them coach you.

■ *Rapport – You have to trust and like this person, and they you.*

Question to yourself: How did you feel about this person when you met them – in the first three seconds? If it was very uncomfortable, do not have them as a coach.

■ *Myth? – Re-read the Myths from page 47 and ask these three questions:*

1   How much do you know about the mind?
2   How many sessions will we need?
3   Do you charge on time, or results?

Because this book will be read by coaches pitching for work, you must decide the 'right' answers to these.

4   *Based on the above, what is the process for choosing a business coach?*

■ Know where you want to go: Know your 'what' – your dream, result and outcome.
■ Know where you are now: Are you in ownership? Are you honest about what is 'right' about you (your strengths, skills and talents)? This will decide if you want to be a pioneer – to boldly go where no one has gone before – or whether you want to follow a proven path … or perhaps something in between.

- Know what you have to do, to get to where you want to go. It is not critical to know this, it is critical to find a coach that will know what steps you need to take to get there.
- Do it! This is what most great business coaches do – they help you to take action. So, they will be a cross between an army sergeant and a cheerleader, and be able to switch between the two at any moment.
- Meet the potential coach. Make the most of this session by asking the questions above and bringing a specific business challenge you face to the table. When you meet them, do they listen to you – really pay you total and absolute attention? Do they speak in plain English with no jargon or mystery? Do they make it absolutely clear that the power in the relationship is with you?
- Engage the coach on the basis of achieving specific results over a set number of sessions. The best coaches will give you access to them between face-to-face sessions and more …

■

Coached by a horse

Knowing that I am pretty open to unusual experiments, my coach once asked whether I would consider an unorthodox coaching session with a new approach. Of course I said yes. We drove out to the country and there I met my new coaching partner. He was a big horse (*very* big – weighing almost a ton to my eight stone frame) and his name was JohnJo.

We studied each other cautiously. Apparently JohnJo was used to working with people, and was extremely sensitive to their energy, motivation and sincerity. My task was to build mutual trust through communication, empathy, and by understanding him and his needs.

I tentatively took JohnJo's lead and took him into the paddock. My first task was simple, or so it seemed. I had to stand in the middle of the paddock and, holding on to his rope, get JohnJo to run in a circle around me. His trainer certainly made it look simple. Yet when I took the rope, I felt very self-conscious – JohnJo quickly sussed this out and, rather than going in a circle, came straight at me forcing me to step back and put my hand out to stop him.

I felt very silly, and self-conscious, and I asked my coach what I should do.

He said he could not tell me, that I had to work it out for myself – however he did give me a hint – he said this:

'Imagine that JohnJo is your team – he needs to believe in you to follow you ... believe all of you – what you say, what you do, how you are. And, most importantly, your focus needs to be on him not on you.' This, then, was to be the theme of the day.

I took hold of the rope again, but this time my focus was on JohnJo. I watched him, I spoke to him, about him. Pointing the direction, talking to him, creating energy behind him with my hand, willing him to go around and around. And soon, I wasn't thinking about myself – I was there mentally and emotionally with JohnJo running around in a perfect circle.

I was there, and nowhere else – it was like the whole world was here in this paddock.

Next, the rope was gone and now it was just me and John-Jo. My new task was to walk him around the paddock – getting him to go where I wanted.

This required communication at its deepest, most empathetic level. I stood next to JohnJo and patted him. I asked him where he wanted to go. As we walked next to each other, I figured out a way to get him to follow – sometimes by gently patting him and talking to him at the same time, sometimes by being more forceful and leaning him in my direction. I stayed attentive to him throughout – working out when he really needed to stop, and when he was trying it on and testing me.

As we did this we became one, with a connecting energy that is difficult to put into simple words. And as this happened, I lost all sense of self-consciousness – I was aware only of JohnJo and what I wanted to get him to do, and what he wanted in return.

As the tasks became more complex, so they became easier, leading to JohnJo choosing to run with me – by walking beside him and then starting to run with him and having him pick up my body energy and also starting to run right next to me.

It was the most rewarding and exhilarating experience feeling this massive horse – ten times my size and power – starting to move at the same pace as me, replicating my tempo and matching my energy …

So what was my learning from this day? The most important one was about the importance of emotional leadership. At the end of the day, words did not matter to JohnJo – he simply did not understand them. What he was reacting to was the strength of my convictions. He was also reacting to the level of my engagement with him and my interest in him – how attentive, how committed and how unselfish I was being with him. How committed I was to him and to doing things together.

And at the end of the day, isn't that what coaching and leadership are all about? So often we hide – behind words, charts, presentations and speeches. But at the end of the day, in front of our teams and with our people, we are in the middle of a paddock, bare and honest. And our success with people is achieved in the same way as my success with JohnJo – by being grounded and confident, by maintaining strength of conviction and resolve and focus, by putting my energy on him (them) vs. myself and focusing solely on achieving success together.

People take more from emotional intuition than from words. So, what we communicate with words matters a lot less than what we communicate with our emotions.

Today, when I am in front of a large group and I feel uncertain or insecure, I think of myself in the middle of that paddock with my smart, beautiful, powerful, giant, silent companion, and I find my grounding, my resolve and my inner strength and emotion to share and channel toward whoever my audience might be …

■

Julia Goldin

■

Journey Three – Your Coaching Relationships

YOU AS COACH

Note: please read this in conjunction with One – Finding a Coach for Yourself

1   *In addition to One, are there any other key skills I need to be a great business coach?*
    Yes – bravery, and lots of it.

It came just 25 minutes into the day. We were at Corporate Headquarters in New York, with the top 50 people of the organization present.

The CEO had just asked if he was a great communicator, and had been greeted by silence. He then said: 'OK, I'll take that as a 'Yes'.'

As the external coach present, in the role of facilitator for the day, I stood up and said: 'Hold on one moment. I would like to see what people feel about the question you asked. Hands up if you feel that Mike is a great communicator.'

Ten hands went up, another five half-up.

I then asked who thought that Mike was not a good communicator at all – the other extreme. Over 20 hands went up – full up.

Given it was a lot more difficult for people to raise their hands the second time than the first, I knew the reviews of the vast majority of the room. So I said: 'OK, let's resolve this.' Mike interrupted and said: 'No, we will not do that.' I turned to him and said: 'You asked for today to be the breakthrough that you wanted, so we will do this – now. We have a choice. We can go there and transform this group and therefore your organization, or not. And if we do this, it will be a sign of massive courage by you, Mike, which I know everyone in this room will respect and admire.'

And so we went there. It was dark, yet as a direct result, that organization turned in its first profit in four years.

Angela Harrington

■

Naked Coaches, and the very best business coaches, are not experts, academics or any kind of guru. They are just ordinary people who have had the great fortune to work with many companies, leaders, and people across the world. From that, they have drawn together the best of the very best ways to create one team. No hype, jargon or mystery; just practical 'how-to's that always work, and produce the results their clients desire.

2 So why don't all business coaches do this?

Three reasons:

- They don't know how to create such an accelerated change, because most leadership providers tell them it is not possible.
- It takes courage to identify and address the real, deeper issues facing a person – such as choice, behaviour and respect.
- Often, a client's priority of running a business takes precedence over running themselves, and yet the first depends on the second.

■

The ice had been melting, but slowly, slowly; I felt I was using a blowtorch against a frozen landscape. What cracked it open was a question (because it's always a question). It shifted the focus from the head to the heart.

'I've noticed you're sad. What are you sad about?'

That was the shift. Permission to have that emotion and to cry.

The ice split. Open water appeared.

Warm wishes,
Michael Bungay Stanier
Canadian Coach of the Year 2006

■

3   The first session

This session is about creating a partnership that you can both work with. You will be asked questions, and you must ask some questions as well. Questions such as:

- Looking at the formula, which parts are you clear about?
- What are your three greatest strengths?
- What is your dream? (If the answer is 'Don't know', ask 'If you did have a dream, what would it be?')
- Do you understand that I stand for YOU, not your goals?
- What is important to you?
- If you could change just one thing in this business, what would it be?

And:

- Can we agree specifically when and how the coaching will happen?
- How would you like to receive your feedback coaching?

■

At the first session, it is important to establish your credibility – and you do this by simply holding up a mirror for the person being coached.

Marc O'Brien

■

4. The proposal for partnership

Coaching partnership for (person being coached) with (business coach)

Results for you and (your organization)
Your true and natural potential will be unleashed, benefiting you and focusing on your (company's) agenda to overcome your biggest challenges, and perform at the very best that you ever have.

We will relate what you do directly to the benefits of (your organization).

The 'what': specifics – I will personally coach you
- To become the master of innovation and change, leading a team that generates ideas, and takes action that leads to real, enduring business value.

Measured by: the Performance Indicators of your team, their perception by your customers – internal and external – and the morale of the team members.

- To be an outstanding communicator at all levels.

Measured by: your ability to build rapport with people, to communicate and lead upwards and to influence at all levels.

- In relationship mastery – how to build immediate rapport with anyone, at any time, and project the gravitas required to confidently operate at any level.

Measured by: we will select three people – one you are close with, one with whom you have a neutral relationship, and one who you often disagree with, before and after the coaching assignment.

- To be totally confident. You will have total and absolute control of your actions in every moment, with any and all fears being removed forever.

Measured by: you.

■ To build a powerful, personal brand within the business world. You will have a crystal clear brand, a unique and powerful business profile, in your own right.

For example, measured by: you will speak at a conference – full of attendees, the number of printed articles in the business press, and the number of hits your name attracts on a search engine of your choice – before and after.

and

■ If you choose, I will include time with you and your partner, including a private one-to-one with your partner, helping them with their personal and business confidence, and overcoming any challenges they may be facing.

The 'how' – in total privacy

■ Four half-days of one-to-one personal coaching in private, planned stages, pre-scheduled at appropriate agreed times, over a 3-month period (start and end months).
■ Four one-hour coaching telephone calls, pre-scheduled at agreed times, over a 3-month period (start and end months).
■ Personal access to coach on a private mobile telephone number.
■ Personal access to coach via a private email address.

Your commitment

■ Time (attendance, attention).
■ Action (you will do what we agree).
■ Honesty (we need the biggest dreams and challenges on the table).

Investment

■ X plus VAT and expenses. Payable as 3 x 1/3 over the three months, with the final payment being subject to ALL results being achieved (as agreed in advance).
■ Be clear on what 'expenses' are.
■ Your name for their name and date.

5 The four sessions ...

This whole book is about the approaches, attitude, trust, dreams, and ownership choices, decisions, commitment and actions that will come out of your four sessions.

Overall:

- Re-read Journey Two – 'Self-coaching' (page 71 ff.). You are now going to coach another person through that same journey.
- Re-read the stuff on 'The place of power' (page 55).
- At the start, clarify the coaching agreement in terms of both of you being absolutely clear what you want to achieve from the relationship, and make sure the person you are coaching knows the power is with them, not you.
- Suspend your ego.
- Be with the other person, totally – they are the most important person on this planet, right now.
- Listen four times as much as you speak – welcome silences.
- Tell stories – use any in this or The Naked Leader books and use your own.

And begin ...

Session One – know where they want to go ...

- Dreams – massive (they do not need to know the 'how' yet – indeed it helps if they do not); and
- Outcomes – clear, concise and compelling. No ambiguity.

... and – know where they are now

- Ownership – ramp up the pain and pleasure until they take true and total ownership (who is the person who is preventing the dream from happening?); and
- Honesty – about their strengths.

Between Sessions One and Two – they attend any christening and funeral (ask permission at the door – you will always be welcome).

Make sure they take ownership for everything. They have access to you and you call them at agreed times.

Session Two – the BIGGIE

- Choices – life-*choosing* not life-*changing*;
- Decisions – now, ensure what they want is a true decision;
- This is a turning point in their life – an absolute commitment to themselves, and to others;
- Make four true decisions: one for themselves, one for someone whose life they touch, one of their team/project and one for their organization – NOW; and
- Check back that they relate to the coaching agreement.

Between Sessions Two and Three, they relax and enjoy having made the decision. They gather strength. They ensure that their teams/projects and all meetings make true decisions – every time. They have access to you and you call them at both agreed and random times.

Note: this is also the time to meet their partner, if agreed in advance. With their partner, you talk through where the coaching is, and you help them as well. Do not share anything that is confidential. I suggest you meet as a three, and then as a two with your coachee's partner.

Session Three – do it!

- Actions – the first action: the 'what', the 'when' and the 'how';
- You tell them how, if they need it – in line with The Deal;
- Ensure they take at least one action, by phone, while you are with them; and
- Conclude with an agreed list of decisions, first actions.

Between Sessions Three and Four – time period of between one week minimum and one month maximum. Daily calls from you and calls from them, whenever they choose. These calls are about the actions (do they take you closer to where you want to go?, etc.) You pile on the 'how-to's, you encourage, you support … and you stalk!

They must not, they will not, give up.

Session Four – the celebration

- ▪ Ensure they know this can all be done, by themselves, without you; and
- ▪ Celebrate together.

Then call them twice in the next week. Invite them to call you any time in the first month after Session Four.

And then your coaching relationship is over.

▪

Toxic coaching

Assisting others to achieve their full potential, cutting through limiting beliefs, opening up new pathways of seeing and helping relationships to flourish are just some of the benefits of an excellent coaching partnership, with the focus being firmly on the client's agenda. Coaching has a beginning, a middle and an end. So what happens when it is the coach that cannot let go of the relationship and the contract is kept going long after it should? This is what can be referred to as 'toxic coaching' – when the needs of the coach start taking precedence over the needs of the person being coached. This can be for a number of reasons: ego, credibility, cash flow, unable to let go ... the list can go on!

Therefore, as a coach, I am driven by ABC – Always Be Contracting. For me, this means not only contracting with the client but also regularly reviewing my own position in the coaching relationship – contracting with myself!

In all my coaching relationships, I regularly ask myself the following questions?

- ▪ Am I giving the client the right level of support for what *they* need now?
- ▪ Is there any evidence of co-dependency in the coaching relationship?
- ▪ Can I clearly see/feel where I am in the coaching cycle?

Coaching relationships are transitory. That's not to say that you cannot reinstate the relationship sometime in the future, when the client faces new challenges or has new goals to pursue, but to believe that coaching is permanent is the start of a toxic coaching relationship. So a coach must be aware that an end to a coaching assignment is as important as the assignment itself!

Judith Underhill
Your Business Matters Limited
www.your-business-matters.com
■

Great coaching questions

Know where you want to go

- What's your biggest dream/What was the biggest dream you had when you were young?
- Why?
- If you had three wishes – one for yourself, one for someone whose life you touch, and one for the world – what would they be?
- What do you want to achieve long term?
- What does success look like for you?
- What's important to you?

Know where you are now

- How much personal control or influence do you have over your goal/dream?
- Do you ever say anything unpleasant behind other people's backs?
- If so, why? If not, really?!?!?
- If I were to ask (boss/spouse/a close colleague) to describe you, what would they say?
- Tell me what is absolutely fantastic about being you?

Know what you have to do, to get to where you want to go

- What were your New Year resolutions?
- How many have been achieved?
- Who can help you achieve this dream?
- Do you have someone whom you can share this dream with, who will laugh at you (very important)?
- Do you have someone close to you whom you can share this dream with, who will not laugh at you (even more important)?

Do it!

- What would be a milestone on the way?
- Descibe a time when you were close to giving up. If you carried on and saw it through, what impact did that have on your life? If you gave up, what impact did that have on your life?
- If things are not going well, what happens to you?
- What commitment, on a 1–10 scale, do you have to taking agreed actions?
- What prevents this from being a 10?
- What could you do to alter or raise your commitment closer to 10?

Journey Three – Your Coaching Relationships

COACHING UPWARDS (INCLUDING CEOs)

Your boss

Whether you call it 'leading,' 'managing' or 'coaching' the key words here are 'your boss'. The politically correct, flat structures of today's businesses have seen that four-letter word almost banned from daily use. However, trust me – everyone has a boss. You may also have semi-bosses who direct you, lead you, motivate you, whatever you.

For them all, there are three cardinal rules:

1   Possession is everything.
2   Possession is everything.
3   Possession is everything.

So, coaching upwards needs a little cleverness and a good sprinkling of politics (just another word for relationships).

Strategy One

When you are with them, one-to-one, listen – really listen, as they will always be talking about their favourite subject (themselves), i.e. whatever they are talking about, they are only doing this from their own personal point of view. This is not an ego thing – it is a human thing. We do not know what it is like to be someone else, so the only person we can talk about with total authority is ourselves.

At some stage they will stop talking (I know, it may be dark by now). You need to keep them talking. You need to discover something here. You need to ask them a question – any question will do, as long as it gets them talking some more.

By the way, you are already now one of their favourite people, because you have shown such a great interest in them.

All the time, you are listening – to what is said and to what is not being said, you are watching their body language, you are totally with them. And all the time you are asking yourself one fundamental question: 'What is my boss's number one need, right now?

Once you have discovered that need, you can simply stand up, lift up your boss and place him/her in your pocket. That is the equivalent of what happens when you offer to help him/her achieve that greatest need. And actually do it!

Strategy Two

Find out the people who impress your boss, and impress them.

■

I always advise ambitious people to identify key stakeholders in the organization, and to build their reputations with them. It is the most powerful route to career success.

Tim Pickard
Area Vice President, International Marketing, RSA Security

■

Strategy Three

Ask your boss what he/she expects of you in your role.

Strategy Four

Be honest, direct and bold. You will be respected, unless your boss is a bully, in which case you must do something about it. You have a right to be treated fairly and with respect.

Strategy Five

Upward leadership and coaching require you to put the organization before yourself. It takes a driving urge to make things happen, and an unflinching willingness to take charge when not fully in command.

■

Picture the scene.

It is Wednesday, 22 August, 2001. The scene is Enron in the USA. Vice President, Sherron Watkins, is meeting Chief Executive, Kenneth Lay. She told him that the company would 'implode in a wave of accounting scandals' from the partnerships that the Chief Financial Officer, Andrew Fastow, was using to hide debt and enrich himself.

Kenneth Lay proved unable to correct the ruinous practice and save the company from bankruptcy just three months later. Regardless of the CEO's decisions, Watkins had courageously acted to avert the impending disaster by thinking as if she were responsible for the company's fate even when the Chief Executive was evidently not.

With thanks to Michael Useem,
Professor of Management and Director of the Leadership Center
Wharton School of the University of Pennsylvania.

■

The CEO

CEOs are human beings just like the rest of us. Know this, and treat them as such, and you have that perfect synergy between life and business coaching that we all seek.

Brian Light
Leadership coach

■

Same strategies as with your boss, with just one difference: you know what is important to your CEO – you know what is keeping him or her awake at night. Because I am about to tell you:

■

In 2002, after many years as a CIO, my focus turned to Chief Executives in private- and public-sector equivalents. I was very fortunate to have a unique 'in' at this level with the success of my book *The Naked Leader*. Within a short time I found myself having trusted conversations with some of the most senior business leaders in the UK, Europe and the world.

And what an eye opener it was. Almost all of them shared my belief that over the last fifteen years, despite billions of global currency being spent on consultancy, change initiatives, technology and training, most organizations have at best stood completely still, and too many people in those organizations remain unfulfilled.

They also agree that during this so-called 'information age' or 'knowledge economy' we have achieved a great deal of … information and knowledge. How much more data do we need before we actually do something with it? Over this period, the more we have talked about how fast change is hitting our organizations, the more things have stayed the same.

Over the last four years I have been asking one overriding question: 'What do you/we need to focus on, and do, to ensure the future is very different from the past?' Over the course of these off-the-record, personal discussions, I have kept an ongoing list of what keeps CEOs awake at night.

Finally, being a CEO is lonely and tough. Everyone thinks they know the answer to everything, and of course they do not. Help CEOs overcome this by taking the actions I suggest below – they are truly unsung heroes.

■

The CEO's top ten issues – from informal chats with 167 CEOs

Note: the one factor that runs through them all is money. Proof of achieving success in any area comes down to proving it in hard financial terms. Every CEO's real number one priority that runs across all of these is personal line of sight of every profit and loss area in the company.

1 *Reputation*
Being, and being seen as, a trusted company in the eyes of stakeholders, customers and the world.

Have a clear Cause – a reason to exist – and ensure everything you are seen to do fits with this reputation. Be a true force for good in your community and in the world. Go beyond corporate and social responsibility, which has become an industry of its own. Action – what is your Cause? And protect your reputation; I have seen millions spent on a brand reputation destroyed by a single television shot.

2 *Leadership*
The next big thing is people – our challenge is that people are waiting for the next big thing.

Your people are not your number one asset; they are your only asset. Action – place leadership at the heart of everything you do – and do it now. Your HR Director becomes Leadership Director, and make sure you have one main leadership provider – yourselves – removing all your external dependence in this vital area.

3 *Customers*
Business is not about making money: it is about delighting customers. The end result is making money.

Make sure your customers love you at an emotional level. Action – ensure that your decision-making authority is at the frontline, with your customer-facing people. The more freedom they have, the happier your customers will be.

4 *Security and compliance*
Be clear on what we need to do, as opposed to what we are told to do.

Have a compliance strategy that is clear. That may sound a contradiction in terms – it is! Challenge it may be, do it anyway. Action – stay out of prison, find out what you must comply with and what doesn't matter. On security, get independent advice that cuts through the nightmares and false stories.

5 *Vision*
Clear, concise and compelling strategy for company.

Have one. Action – ensure everyone in your organization knows it, and knows how what they personally do relates to this strategy. Anything you do that does not help you move closer to your vision, stop doing it. You will stop over a third of your work and create a refreshing clarity.

6 *IT must deliver …*
At last – and release value
from existing systems.

IT has not delivered – it has cost millions and is
a liability in most organizations. Action – ensure
you have the right CIO in place, key skills being 1)
business, 2) always deliver, and 3) leadership. And
forget Prince2: successful projects are all about
people, and very little to do with process.

7 *Agility*
Speed of company.

Action – make true decisions. When you decide
on something, stick to it and don't keep debating
and discussing as you look for the perfect answer
– there isn't one. Discuss, make a decision, and
take a first action. If it takes you forward, great; if
not, then do something else.

8 *Wellness and balance*
Too much stress, too many
lost days, too many not
performing.

Action – if you do 5 and 7 you will free up a lot
of stress. Ensure people know where to go to
when they feel things are getting on top of them.
Support people when they are down and they will
look after you when they are well. And take your
own personal balance seriously: spend time with
your children and your partner. You will regret
not doing so in your final minutes on this earth, I
promise you.

9 *Personal legacy*
'I will leave this organization
in a better state than when I
arrived.'

Action – decide how you want to be remembered
in your organization. Write it down. Have a
successor identified as soon as possible, and
ensure you are totally dispensable as soon as
possible. It's the only way to be indispensable.

10 *Know what we know*

We have plenty of knowledge in our organization
– it is inside people's heads and hidden in our
systems. What do we know? How can we find
out what we need to know? Action – transform
your communication of knowledge by finding
out where people go to find things out.
Document these communication centres – it's
the 'pull' reverse of what we are often told about
communicating (push).

And there is another one: loneliness. Your CEO is probably very lonely
– so go have a chat …

When I joined my new firm in February I quickly realized that the firm could achieve more. So in July, I revised the firm's performance target along with the promise that I would auction my cherished BMW 5 series if the target was not met. A firm-wide bonus – equal payments to everyone from executive to cleaner was implemented alongside the *Save my Car* campaign. This year the firm grew by 16%, its best result for 18 years. The atmosphere was electric too.

The car was saved. The charity will receive its donation from the firm instead and everyone one else gets £639 each plus a day off.

In the words of Derek Trotter: 'Everyone's a winner.'

Glyn Morris

Journey Three – Your Coaching Relationships

ONE TEAM, ONE VISION

One Team, One Vision is written as a 'do-it' section – apply it as you read it; a specific how-to.

1   Know this

It is absolutely critical for your teams to be as one, with one vision, if you are to achieve success in projects or as an organization.

2   Givens

- People can 'belong' to more than one 'team' for a project or an organization to be successful – ensure people understand and accept this, and you will remove internal team rivalries.
- So, 'team' means any group of people working together to achieve a particular result, over any period of time.
- You can make this happen if you so choose.
- Everyone involved must have completed Journey Two – 'Self-coaching'.

3   The best of the very best

This works for every team. It is most powerful when facilitated by some-one who is outside the team, who will not shy away from more challeng-ing issues. This can be someone inside or outside your company, with my recommendation that it is someone from inside your organization.

If you would like to be trained and accredited in doing this, email me: david@nakedleader.com or call 0044–1483–766502 and ask about our in-company accreditation programme.

▪

Coaching can, and must, continue after projects are complet-ed. I am involved in a major project this year (2007) and, in February, I was inspired by the Oscars to do something new. Film credits list all the key people involved in a film, how often do we do this in business?

When a succesful project is delivered, how often does every-one involved get acknowledged and thanked?

Not often enough.

So, I am keeping a list of everyone who has helped me and the project in any way, and will maintain this list as we progress through develpment and on to delivery. Not to work out who to blame if it goes wrong (it won't), but to make sure that I remember who to thank personally for all their help.

And, in my Oscar speech for the Best Motion Picture in Project Delivery, I will name every one of them.

Phil Jones

▪

How to achieve one team, with one vision

The results

To be one team, with one vision and one voice
- ▪ Absolute openness and honesty – putting respect before friend-ship;
- ▪ No more backstabbing – from now on, if you are going to stab anyone, make it in the stomach not in the back;

- One voice to the outside world – collective responsibility always, no exceptions;
- The team is built on, welcomes, and uses each other's strengths;
- Regular openness, especially on what is going well; and
- Transformed leadership, decision-making and behaviours.

1 Set the agenda

This activity is designed to enable everyone to understand what success means to him or her, and to pay total and absolute attention to another human being. Absolute attention. That means listening, not just hearing. This, by itself, is the biggest compliment we can pay another human being: truly valuing what they have to say. Listen to their words and, more importantly, be aware of their body language and movement.

This activity is also designed to help them understand what beliefs or people are stopping them fulfilling their potential.

▪

Ask people to pair with someone (if there are odd numbers, you will need one 'three') that they do not work closely with on a day-to-day basis, perhaps from another area of the organization. This person becomes your buddy in the team, and as you don't work closely together day-to-day, that destroys the excuse about silos, as the pairings will cut across these silos.

Each pair/three considers these two questions:
1 What is your biggest dream/hope/ambition/result for the team?
2 What is the single biggest obstacle or challenge that is preventing it from happening?

They are also told that when they share their thoughts, they will share them *as if* they are the other person – so they will become the other person. This adds to the power because now people will really listen – they will have to!

Outcomes:
- Buddies in place – to help, support, advise and stalk!
- Silos destroyed.
- The agenda is set around day-to-day issues.
- The focus is on the key dreams and biggest challenges.
- People listen and pay attention.

- People have an understanding of each other's points of view.
- It is fascinating (and unnerving) to hear someone else being us. It also provides an incredible insight as they will say what they heard, which may not necessarily be what we said!
- A lot of fun as some people will impersonate others as in *Stars in Their Eyes.*

People then share the biggest dreams and challenges (if the team is big, put them on a time limit). For the 'three', all buddies to each other: A reports back as B, who reports back as C, who reports back as A.

Record the dreams and challenges – one on each flipchart. If something is repeated, add an asterisk next to the same point, and a second if it is repeated again, and so on.

And ask questions – you as facilitator, and of each other. You can be as probing as you like, as you are really asking the team member themselves, via their buddy. The most powerful questions are these:

- Why have you not done anything about this before?
- What happened when you raised this issue with X?
- Who? (to ask when people say 'The trouble with X department ... ')

After everyone has spoken, ask if anyone feels they have been misrepresented. Then report back *as if* you were the other person, when you will share your dreams, your ambitions, and other delegates can ask questions of you. Ask the group how it felt to be someone else.

2   The formula for guaranteed success

Go through the formula:

Know where you want to go – dream and outcome
Ask people to do continuous writing on what is possible for the team (see page 66).

Know where you are now – ownership/accountability and strengths
The key here is simple – to agree that no one in the team will ever say

anything behind each other's backs that they would not say to their faces. This is a given, and must be accepted at an emotional level. If everyone simply nods, they will not do it. If anyone suggests they are already doing this, just ask them if there is anyone in the team that they do not particularly 'get on with'. If they say 'Yes', ask them what happened when they shared that with that person, in private. People must buy into this at an emotional level. Everyone must buy into it.

Another way:

▪

One of my most powerful experiences of coaching was from my friend Peter. He asked me to consider what was most important to me, and write this on five points of a star. He asked me to consider in which areas I could be 'brilliant', and to work out how I could achieve 'brilliance', quite specifically, in these.

The power of this is combining ability and personal values in emotive terms, using metaphor. I should not accept merely good as being enough. Peter helped me challenge myself to focus where I am already competent and I really *want* to make a difference. The combination of confidence and desire to succeed that this frame of reference brings is hugely powerful.

Elsa Critchley

▪

Know what you have to do, to get to where you want to go – choices and true decisions

Ask people to look at their dream, their result, their 'what' and to make a true decision – in other words, to decide what they are going to achieve as an individual and as a team, and to close off all other possibilities.

3   Removing final excuses

▪ *Been there, done that – doesn't work.*
  We have all been on long, drawn out, and sometimes boring leadership events. Some of these set strategies, which we then printed up as poster-sized mission statements, put up in meeting rooms, and then forgot all about (if you have a mission statement, write it down now).

▪ *We have something missing.*
As a team, it helps us to believe that we do not have all the key skills/talents that we need – it means we can make excuses forever.

▪ *Too many actions to do – we are busy enough already.*
Identify the top three decisions that you must make to be one team with one vision – three only.

▪ *We don't know what success looks or feels like.*
You soon will.

▪

Split the team into four groups and ask them to nominate a facilitator.

Share this brief with each of the groups in turn, with the strict instruction that they must not share their brief with any other group, until you ask them to. None of the groups must know what any of the other groups are working on.

You share:

▪ Group One – What is the dream/vision/purpose for our team? – in inspiring, clear, simple terms. A vision that really inspires and excites.

▪ Group Two – What are the key skills and behaviours (12 of each) we need to be successful as a team?

▪ Group Three – What are the specific, exact first actions we need to take, to be successful as a team?

▪ Group Four – Once we have achieved success as a team, what will that feel like for us? What will it look like from outside the team, and for our customers?

Tell each group they have six minutes to do it.

What is really going on here is …

Four different groups have six minutes to focus on a different, complementary area, without any group knowing what any other group is doing! The six minutes is chosen to ensure instinct, emotion and agreement overcome analysis, logic and disagreement.

Ask each facilitator to nominate someone in their group to feedback to the wider group, chosen by who was quietest in the group. Feedback takes place in the order One, Two, Three, Four, with you revealing that group's brief as you reach their number.

▪

Outcomes from Session Three:

- A clear, concise and compelling vision/dream/purpose;
- Fun, exciting and interactive – boring mission statements, eat your heart out!
- A clear list of skills/behaviours (and they will all be within the team – proving that 'we can't' is an excuse);
- The skills will also predominantly be leadership/softer – showing that technology is not important: it is what we do with it that counts;
- Clear focus on first actions and on results/wider organization – leading to improved bottom line and customer service; and
- All excuses removed.

4   The fastest way to make any change in this team

Share the three essential 'truths', in an interactive way, of how we are as human beings:

- When we believe something to be true, we see the world in that way (see 4a on the next page).
- We automatically move in the direction of our most dominant thoughts – what we think about, we are (see pages 148–152).
- Our minds cannot tell the difference between something that happens in 'reality' and something we imagine with emotional intensity (see pages 148–152).

4a When we believe something to be true, we see the world in that way.

■

Saboteur game – Lego

Objective: To demonstrate that when we believe something to be true, we see the world in that way.

Play games concurrently – maximum of 12 per game
Preparation.

You need :

- Two very close rooms, A and B – or one room A, separated in two.
- One Lego structure – ideally randomly built.
- Duplicate pieces – including an identical base – in a bag or box.
- Have Lego structure in corner of Room A.
- Have bag of Lego bits in Room B (or other corner of A – inside bag).
- You also need small square pieces of paper folded up.
- If you choose to have a Saboteur, one of the pieces should say 'It's You', the rest 'X'.
- If you choose not to have a Saboteur all will have an 'X'.

Instructions:

Ask everyone to gather together in Room B. Explain the following key points in your own way:

'As you know, the NLE Top Leadership Two Days is a breakthrough event. However, we also have to include one team game. I'm sorry about this and we will get it over with, as fast as possible!

Next door there is a structure. Inside this bag, you have everything you need to achieve your aim/goal, which is to build an identical structure to the one next door, in 20 minutes.

The rules:

- This is the only time in the two days when you must not cheat!
- Only one member of the team is allowed outside of this room, at a time (it therefore follows that only one member of the team can be in the other room, with the structure, at any one time).

■ You can only communicate with each other inside this room – no communication can take place outside of this room, or with anyone outside of this room.

■ The structure next door cannot be moved.

■ You cannot move anything out of this room, other than yourselves.

■ You cannot write anything down.

■ Everyone in the team must be involved in the game – unless at least two other members decide they should not be.

■ I am allowed to make up rules on an ongoing basis, as you seem a very clever group.

Your time starts now. Oh, hold on … Sorry, I am so sorry; there is one extra thing I completely forgot to tell you.

■ One of you is a Saboteur – I do not know who it is, and neither do you; only he or she will know.'

Hand out papers – collect them again. Make sure no one sees anyone else's paper, of course!

'OK, I am now talking directly to the Saboteur – the others must not listen! On each of these pieces of paper was written something – either an 'X' or an 'It's You'. If you have an 'X', you are a team member; if you have 'It's You', you are a team member and THE SABOTEUR. And by the way, I am NOT the Saboteur – as I did not have a piece of paper!

It is the Saboteur's job to ensure that you do not succeed in your task. To do this they may cheat, lie, and generally cause mayhem. He or she will only succeed if the rest of you do not achieve your task.

Warning to the Team: as well as completing the task, you must gather evidence as you do so, as to the identity of the Saboteur.

Warning to the Saboteur – the Team will do everything they can to identify you. They may ask questions like 'This is a trusted group, are you the Saboteur?' – remember, that is just desperation, they do not know who you are, so enjoy yourself.'

Answer any questions (the above list covers every question I have ever been asked). During the exercise, wander around observing. Two key points:

1   Because you have positioned the completed structure in an awkward position, very quickly it will be touched. Wait a few minutes – stop the game and say very grandly: 'I have to tell you the structure has been moved. I've restored it to its original position.'

2   There is no chance of them completing the task in 20 minutes – so add five minutes on after about 10 minutes, announcing that: 'The Saboteur is doing such a good job that I have added five minutes on to your time.' Continue to periodically mention the Saboteur – e.g. 'The Sab. is doing a great job,' or 'Remember, you may want to start gathering evidence on who the Saboteur is,' etc.

At the end of the game, no one must speak with any of the others. Ask everyone to go back to the main room. Get a piece of paper and write down each and every person they feel could have been the Saboteur, and ask them to add evidence that made them think it.

Take both structures – the before and after – through with you.

Team members must not put their name on the paper (to avoid fights breaking out!)

Read out the papers – how the facilitator does this is up to them.

Key point: when we believe something to be true, we see the world in that way.

Discussion – have a laugh and reveal who the Saboteur actually is.

▪

5   Make a true decision, *as if* it has already happened

The fastest way to make any change in your life
In your own words, the facilitator must get this across – these are mine:

▪

We are human beings, not human doings. We will know at any moment of our lives whether we are 'being' or whether

we are 'doing' by how we feel. The most natural feeling in
the world is total and absolute one-ness. Inner peace.

■

Too often we live our lives in reverse. 'If I get promoted, then I will
do my job better because I will have value and then I will BE a better
leader.' Or, 'If I get the big job, car and house, I can drive around looking important, entertain lavishly, then I really will be somebody.'

Absolute calm is restored into our lives when we decide to live
our lives in the grandest version of our grandest vision. This does not
mean we walk around with a 'holier than thou', arrogant expression
– quite the reverse. It is the difference between knowing and telling;
it is the difference between self and ego. Absolute calm comes from
within, and when we move from *get >do >be* to *be >do >get*.

How can we do this? How long will it take us? The answer is,
one single heartbeat. In the moment we take in, embrace, and make
happen the following life-transforming statement.

We already know that:

- We automatically move in the direction of our most dominant
  thoughts;
- When we believe something to be true, we see the world in that
  way; and
- Our minds cannot tell the difference between something that
  happens in 'reality' and something we imagine with emotional
  intensity.

From this, the single most powerful way to make any change in your
life is to act *as if* that change has already been made.

WOW!!!

Acting 'as if' is the complete opposite of everything I ever previously learned about success. By the way, it has many other names. If I
was out to really impress you I would tell you what psychologists call
it. Oh, all right then. Wait for it: 'Autogenic conditioning'. Just a small
'wow' this time. It's also known as 'fake it till you make it'.

And that is all irrelevant to the possibilities it opens up in our
lives, and the fact that our lives can be transformed so fast.

■

I have seen a father reconnect with his daughter, just by thinking 'as if'.

They had not been close for many years, she was at University and he was working every hour there was. He wanted to re-ignite their relationship, their friendship, and their love. And so he wrote his outcome: 'I will have a close, loving relationship with Rebecca, based on mutual trust, openness and friendship.'

I asked him to word it in the present, in the *as if*.

He said OK and wrote:

'I will have a close, loving relationship with Rebecca, based on mutual trust, openness and friendship.'

His brain would not allow him to do it. After all, we all know that success is something that happens in the future, it cannot happen NOW. Success is something we all aspire to; it cannot be here, with us, NOW. After all, it takes time to achieve, often many years of grind and hardship, it cannot arrive NOW.

It can, and it does, and it did for my friend. I took a pen, and crossed out just one word.

'I ~~will~~ have a close, loving relationship with Rebecca, based on mutual trust, openness and friendship.'

And his life changed forever. One pen stroke made in one heartbeat.

He looked at the piece of paper and left the room, mobile phone in hand. I knew who he was going to call … that was four years ago, and I am delighted, and humbled, to report that father and daughter (now 22) are doing well, and two people could not be closer.

▪

Let us look at what happened here:

From 'I will have a close, loving relationship with Rebecca, based on mutual trust, openness and friendship' to 'I have a close, loving relationship with Rebecca, based on mutual trust, openness and friendship'. Any judgement of 'right' or 'wrong' was bypassed and a new reality born. Put quite simply, as human beings. And he took immediate action. NOW. After all, as he has such a relationship, NOW, he will act in a certain way.

I have had the privilege to work with many thousands of leaders (i.e. people) throughout the world. From these I have heard many hundreds of amazing stories, including:

- The woman who announced on day one that she had the worst memory in the world, and after 'as if', she had the best memory (and is now a memory champion).
- The team who had never been as one. They had always argued, been in dispute and had no respect for each other. A week-long team-building event did not help, either. And then they all decided to act *as if* they were one team. And guess what?

And my personal favourite:

- The nephew of a very close friend of mine, a boy of nine who was very unhappy and no-one could reach the root cause. When he came to visit us once, I asked him if he would like to play a game – called 'The Happy Game' – in which we both have to act *as if* we are very happy (deliriously so, on this occasion). We told each other jokes and quickly reached the stage of laughing just for the sake of it. After we finished, he was in a far better state than when we started, because it is simply not possible to act happy without actually *being* happy.

When we use 'as if' in our lives, we move from *get>do>be* to *be>do>get*.

There is one other, very powerful element to all of this. In our lives, there are three aspects that determine if we can achieve something, be successful, and be more than what we have become. These are:

- Our experience
- Our knowledge
- Our imagination

Which plays a bigger part? Funnily enough, if you ask people with experience, they say 'experience', and if you ask people with knowledge (say, newly qualified students) they say 'knowledge'.

Actually, while these are both important, it is our *imagination* that plays the biggest single part in our achievements, our leadership and in our lives, by far. If you doubt the power of our imaginations, go and see a horror film. You know the story is not real, that they are actors wearing masks, so why are you clinging onto the person next to you? (Very embarrassing if you do not know them!) Or … read a book, watch TV, have a dream, or …

It is absolutely critical that the facilitator shares personal experiences and examples here:

Be the best now

▪

One can never consent to creep when one feels an impulse to soar.

Helen Keller

▪

If your team is to be and act as the best team now, then everyone within it owes it to themselves, and to the team, to be the best they can now.

- ▪ Again, we need to reverse the *get>do>be* formula. We cannot be the kind of person we want to be, or the team we want to be, until we have *the resources* that enable us to. And by being and acting as that person or team from day one, we start to achieve the kind of results we dream of and thereby naturally gather the resources we require.
- ▪ To make sure that this image of the best you is 'real' and compelling, it must be *OWNED by everyone in the team*. OWNED:

Own	You must own this image. What **you** want to be, not what someone else wants you to be. It must come from the heart.
Want	It must be you feeling good and acting positively. Sort out the negative aspects of your life before they take you over.
Now	It must be you in the here and now, not some vague, ill-defined future that never arrives.
Emotional	It should be an image of yourself that excites you, that engages your emotions and passions, that makes you burn to be that you.
Defined	Fill in all the details, and make it come alive. What are you doing? How are you feeling? What are the colours, smells, sensations?

6 'How-to's

Select and share the most powerful, relevant 'how-to's from Journey Five (see page 247), or decide some for yourselves, or go to www.nakedleader.com/howto and ask any question – you will receive many 'how-to's in return.

7 The moment of truth

▪

Buddies and commitment – includes break

Interactive with Buddies – Are you ready to make a true decision for us to be a team? And to close off all other possibilities. If you are not, why not? Your buddy questions and probes to establish if it really is a true decision, and is worded in the present, *as if* it has already happened. The buddies agree how they will keep in contact with each other, and continue to help and encourage.

Now – the holy grail of teamwork. Each person looks at the biggest challenge that they shared in the morning – the one preventing their dream from happening. They take personal ownership of it with the commitment of the first action – the first 'how-to' that they will take, and when.

Note: the most frequent excuse by a 'neg' will be something like 'I will do it, but I am not convinced everyone else will.' In which case, as their buddy, you decide how daring you are: very daring? Ask: 'Who?'

▪

8 Final session – team share

Ask everyone to write down one amazing strength/attribute/ quality about everyone in the team, including themselves. These are written on adhesive notes, one for each person, so that on a course of 12 people, each person will end up with 12 separate adhesive notes, each with one inspiring and amazing comment on it.

Sit in a horseshoe, and start with the person on the horseshoe's right (your left if you are facing them as a facilitator). That team member stands up, shares what is amazing about themselves, and then looks at the number two – the person who was sitting to their left, who then shares what is amazing about the person standing up – number one. The person standing listens with total attention, says thank you – then person three shares what they have written about person one, and so on as set out on the next page.

After they have spoken, they stick their adhesive note onto the person, so that everyone has a lasting reminder of their experience.

■

It is powerful beyond description, stays in the memory forever and is without doubt the most powerful way to close any leadership event.

Sequence for team share

Team of twelve sitting in a horseshoe thus:

1 2 3 4 5 6 7 8 9 10 11 12

Order of sharing – to ensure everyone goes first, last and in every other position, and is thus always just spoken or about to speak and thus involved

Listening (Standing)	Speaking
1	1
1	2
1	3
1	4
1	5
1	6

1	7
1	8
1	9
1	10
1	11
1	12
2	2
2	3
2	4
2	5
2	6
2	7
2	8
2	9
2	10
2	11
2	12
2	1
3	3
3	4
And so on until …	
12	12
12	1
12	2
With the final interaction being	
12	11

Do it!

For the team you are in, write down here each person's greatest strength

Name	Strength

Now, don't wait for a session like team share. Go share now …

Do it!

Make different choices in your teams and projects

The more you do in the third column in the following table on disablers, the higher you will rise in any organization, and the better prepared you will be to take your place as a Director, with board-level responsibility.

Disabler	Choice One	Choice Two
'How can I write a departmental strategy when we don't have a business one?'	Wait for a business strategy to be written. Grow cobwebs as you wait.	Go to your CEO and offer to help write such a strategy, facilitating input from all areas in the organization.
'Our projects are not clearly prioritized. How can I be expected to plan resources?'	Ask the CEO/Board to prioritize projects, please. And when they don't, simply ask them again. When they finally do it, watch how many will be priority one.	Do it yourself, on the basis of the deliverable business value that each will provide. Every project must deliver such measurable value. Present at Board meeting. After the arguments subside you will have a prioritized list.
'We need to innovate more – how can I find time to do this?'	Never innovate. Worse still, hold an innovation session outside of day-to-day work, and stack up hundreds of ideas, adding to work pressure.	Innovate within the projects you are working on by focusing on what you want to achieve (dreams and outcomes), not want you want to avoid (fears and risk).
'My key suppliers are at the root of many of my problems – they need to be brought into line.'	Wave the contract at them – no, hit them with it. Tell them that as the customer you are always right and, most importantly, threaten them (professionally of course).	Take the supplier out for a drink, and each take five minutes to share, openly, professionally and privately, what has gone wrong and what you most need from each other.
'More and more decisions on my team and projects are being made outside of my team. Sometimes I am not even consulted.'	This is totally unacceptable. Go to the managers concerned and make it clear that you or your people must be involved in any and all key decisions.	If you are not advised, then you are not trusted. Most organizations are federal and don't run on hierarchal lines. Embrace and encourage this, and lead the process as a facilitator and business leader.
'You say that to get promoted onto the Board my CEO has to like and trust me, yet I don't like or trust them. What can I do?'	Make a long and logical presentation to them about how personalities should not come into such decisions, and that it is far more important that your area is represented at board level. Good luck with that one.	Start liking and trusting them, or find another job.
'One person in my organization seems to have a go at me/us no matter what we do – and they are a key influencer. It is getting me down.'	Show them the last three Service Level Agreements and availability/project success figures and tell them to get off your back. Then ignore them.	Invite them to work in your department for a period, asking for their help and experience to improve what you do.

▪

I was a project manager for an international charity, planning and leading a team in Zimbabwe made up of young people from the UK. Our objective – to create an ecological map for a newly formed conservancy. This meant sending teams into the bush and co-ordinating their movements, and enabling re-supply of provisions. They braved heat, drought, floods and generally tough conditions. I would call this coaching in challenging conditions!

One day, a rendezvous failed. A team of four lost! We organized a search party, and for three days we searched and feared the worst. During that time we all came together as one – internal squabbles were forgotten; we communicated brilliantly, (somehow). We all had a focus as one, (somehow). Hey, even the insect bites didn't hurt anymore, somehow.

We found them alive and well and, when we reflected on it all, we realized that if we always choose to behave as as a crisis seems to make us behave, we can be as one, always.

Jack Noble
Fujitsu

▪

Do it!

Or sing a song:

▪

All together now – I promise to sing if you do. Oh, OK then …

Que sera sera

When I was just a little girl
I asked my mother: 'What will I be?'
Will I be pretty?
Will I be rich?
Here's what she said to me:

(Chorus)
Que sera sera
Whatever will be, will be
The future's not ours to see
Que sera sera
What will be, will be.

When I grew up and fell in love
I asked my sweetheart, what lies ahead?
Will we have rainbows
Day after day?
Here's what my sweetheart said:

(Chorus)

Now I have children of my own
They ask their mother, what will I be?
Will I be handsome?
Will I be rich?
I tell them tenderly:

(Chorus)

▪

I know team leaders who ask people to sing this song, and then ask them to tear up the song sheets and throw them at you. Great fun, and making the point that our future is up to us.

Journey Four

– Be a Truly Authentic Organization

Journey Four – Be a Truly Authentic Organization

THE FUTURE – NOT WHAT IT USED TO BE

Journey Four starts with 'what' and moves to the 'hows'. All the 'how-to's in this book can be used to achieve a truly authentic organization.

Make your organization a Next Business Great in the 21st century

Business coaching is always about people and their business/career/organization. People are representatives or champions of their organization. Coaching them is an access tool into their organizational culture and business ethic. The coaching serves as a tool to inspire their organization, through them, in developing a future relationship or business development opportunity. They need to be 'coached' in 'delivering' a message back to their colleagues who may be budget holders or gatekeepers.

Ultimate success in business coaching comes down to knowing the objective. Know that objective … from all perspectives, theirs and yours.

Mike Sharkey

Note: this can apply, and be adapted, to any and every organization in the world, large/small, public/private, company or school/college.

Whenever I use the word business, company, or similar, the principles apply – to any organization, anywhere on earth.
We have spent much energy, time and money, looking for success, answers and leadership from outside, from without, when they have always been inside of us, from within.

▪

> Everything you need, to be anything you want, is waiting and within …

▪

In the future, organizations will have fewer opportunities to grow through mergers and acquisitions. The main route for growth will be organic, from within. This will require a radical new approach to leadership.

1 A call to action

The Next Business Age is a call to action for all leaders, of all companies, who choose to create a truly enlightened organization, and be a business great in the 21st century.

The Next Business Age is a choice, not an answer. The great fallacy of 'best-practice' is that what works in one organization will work in another. Why would it? So, the Next Business Age is a blueprint of practical ideas, beliefs, behaviours and actions that can be put into immediate practice. It is what any organization, large or small, public or private, thriving or struggling, could look like, if the people inside those organizations make certain choices.

▪

> James Dyson quotes George Bernard-Shaw: 'All great truths begin as blasphemies.' The problem is people don't like blasphemies at first. New thoughts are the lifeblood of business, but they always start as uncomfortable blasphemies.
>
> So how do you get them off the ground? How do you get the people in your company to believe in your particular blasphemy – your particular innovation? The key is to remember that people don't believe in ideas, they believe in people who believe in ideas. Declare your blasphemy with the clarity and conviction of your favourite hero and it has a chance of sticking.
>
> *Chris Satterthwaite*
> *Chief Executive*
> *Chime Communications plc*

▪

2 Less insight; more eyesight

The Next Business Age is not based on academic research. It is a practical action and belief document, based on 30 years' experience working in, for and with many hundreds of organizations and many thousands of leaders around the world.

The Next Business Age is a 'what', and not a 'how'. 'How' is the single most damaging three-letter word, the single, shortest word that has killed so many dreams and ambitions. Each 'what' in this document suggests three ideas/actions/'how's, and for each one of these, there are thousands more.

As an individual, as a team or an organization, you only have to know the 'what' first; you do not need to know the 'how' yet. The reason for this is the ultimate irony of success, consultancy and personal and professional books: there is too much 'success' – too many 'how's going around, far too many for us to evaluate and choose from. And, too often, after we have chosen one, it does not work in its entirety, and neither will it ever do so. The idea that one single person, or company, or book, has the monopoly on what to do, to make your dream come true, is a complete myth.

3 It's about you

The Next Business Age belongs to no one; it belongs to everyone. Its ideas and actions are open and available to all. And that includes you. Whether you choose to take action, to make your company great, is entirely up to you.

4 Our time is short ...

I do not seek long and detailed debate on whether this blueprint is 'right' or 'wrong', for two reasons.

Firstly, in the global business communities, we have talked for too long. We have talked about new ideas, and debated what we 'should' be doing for what seems like forever. We have been advised by consultants, told what to do by people who should know better, we have wasted much time, and opportunity. The more change we craved, the more we stood still. Now it is time for action.

Secondly, we always seek evidence for what we believe to be true. Within three months of publication, this blueprint will generate literally thousands of emails, contributions and proof that it is 'right', and an equal volume that it is 'wrong'. One of the core premises of writing this document is that there is no 'right' or 'wrong' anymore, outside the moral sense. There is only what takes you closer to where you want to go – and who you want to be – and what takes you further away.

5 The four powers of next business greats

The Next Business Age does not begin or end on a certain date. It starts whenever you choose it to start, and in the moment you decide to make different choices over the four areas that have not delivered real, measurable value over the last 15 years:

- Your employees – an organization's only asset, indeed, they *are* your organization;
- Your customers and potential customers – its livelihood;
- Your shareholders and investors – those that have taken financial risks for success; and
- Technology – what it does, and the value it brings to the above, not what it is.

6 Imagine ...

Imagine a future compelling in vision and full of unlimited possibilities, wonderful excitement, and massive rewards.

Imagine no more. You are capable of achieving anything you wish, and more. When people awaken their potential, their imaginations, and their energies, the results are astounding. And it can happen to anyone, any team, any company, for any one person, group of people, or organization. Once you embrace this idea and put it into action, you hold in your hands a power that is quite awesome.

It is time to reawaken your people – a resource, an investment, a power that has been dormant for far too long – for the benefit of all

– you, your organization, and our world. I say this to all leaders who are ready to achieve a professional and personal success they had previously never dreamed possible.

Where has all the money gone?

Over the last 15 years, organizations have spent billions of global currencies on training, technology, consultancy and so-called change initiatives, and yet the vast majority of these organizations have, at best, stood completely still and many people remain unfulfilled.

Over this time, in the UK alone, we have 'invested' over £200 billion in business consultancy – and yet over 60 of the companies that were in the FTSE 100 in 1990 are now no longer there. The top 100 listed UK companies in 1990 were virtually the same as they were in 1984 – the year the FTSE 100 was formed. Yet over the following ten years, 67 of the top 100 companies have either disappeared, been radically changed, or have just been displaced from the FTSE 100 list.

Only 33 companies survive on the list. This has happened during the so-called 'information age' or 'knowledge economy'.

In addition, over that time, public perception of business, in particular big business, is one of greed, corruption, poor service and mistrust, and people and the media have no shortage of examples: Enron, Andersen Consulting, Worldcom, and all of those organizations that reward failure with large pay-offs. Popular culture often derives its opinions from film and books. Increasingly, businesses and business leaders are portrayed in such media as corrupt, even evil.

The result from the last 15 years has been a suspicion of companies and their leaders, in their motives, their ethics and their policies. In a 2004 global survey of over 100,000 people, only two business leaders were nominated as amongst the top 50 greatest leaders.

Most business leaders are entirely ethical, contributing much money to good causes and placing compliance and corporate and social responsibility at the very top of their corporate agendas. However, perception is all, particularly when fuelled by a global media that needs a good story. And ethical, trust-focused business leaders are not a mass-market story.

And it's not just 'big' or established, well-known companies. This scenario is all too familiar to so many people:

Entrepreneur starts business

Is successful. Makes money. Helps others. Develops the business and not himself. Keeps things close to his chest. Has people who too readily say Yes. Still makes money. Becomes very introspective. Performance stutters. Tiredness creeps in. Strategic direction and daily focus slips and is lost. Clarity of thinking is lost. Starts being outperformed. Has to focus on finance so moves service and society to lower priorities. Makes less money and doesn't know why. Has to restructure. Wonders what has gone wrong and what it's all about.

With thanks to TEC International
www.teconline.com

■

The Last Business Age – what has gone wrong?

What has the information age delivered?

Cash over cause
- A focus on cost reduction and bottom line only, at the expense of purpose, something to stand for. What does your organization stand for? What are your values? Ask these questions of different people and you may get many different answers.
- Failure has been too often rewarded – shareholders have had enough and such shareholders have new levels of control and power.
- Business has not perceptibly helped our world, even though many have. Global surveys consistently show that people have had enough of capitalism and greed – and in too many countries and societies, making profit has become synonymous with, at best, suspicious activities and, at worst, breaking the law.

Confusion over clarity

- The 'change agenda' has delivered many things; sadly lasting change is not one of them. It has delivered data and knowledge, which has been overwhelming, and at times led to chaos, with change for change's sake, an initiative-a-day building on and often at odds with existing initiatives (and being damaging and destructive about the previous initiative's value), all with little heed on the impact on your customers or people.
- Few people inside many organizations are clear on its vision and strategy.
- Empowerment and flat structures mean well, yet they have not helped clarify who does what in an organization, who is accountable, and how people's daily jobs relate to the bottom line.

Change over choice

- As people, we don't like change – yet we love to change other people. People will only ever do something to the best of their ability for one reason, and one reason alone: because they want to. It is time to move beyond 'change programmes' to 'choice programmes'.
- Another challenge is that 'change initiatives' are so boring (wouldn't you rather have deep root canal surgery than read another manual on Total Quality Management?), irrelevant (what has an academic tome on change got to do with our organization?) and totally mistrusted (many companies hid behind change initiatives to make people redundant).
- Organizations are changing all the time – in day-to-day service and operations. Too many 'change initiatives' focus on aspects of change that are unrelated to day-to-day activities, creating a great irony – these initiatives have actually led to *less* change happening in the most important and critical parts of our organizations.

Convenience over customers

- Over the last 14 years, organizations have often put their own structures, methods and processes – the way they do things – before the needs of their customers. Their ways of working have become inflexible and cannot cope with their customers' changing needs and increasing demands. The problem here is that, while how we operate as an organization is important, it is not how our customers judge us. Their opinion of us is decided not by what we do, but by what they think we do. It has not helped us that too often our internal processes and procedures are used as a reason (excuse) for not providing great customer service.

■ As organizations have become more complex, so the need for order and structure has increased, so we have an idea of who does what. Unfortunately, such an approach has often been on what makes an organization work efficiently (i.e. knowing how to do things), as opposed to working effectively (i.e. knowing what to do).

■ During this information age, with most knowledge being held centrally, that is where most decisions are being made, at the expense of front-line decision-making freedom, and co-ordination of customer service. This has had two major and devastating consequences: people providing a service directly to customers cannot, or feel they cannot, make critical decisions; and, just as the marketing department is sending out a brochure to encourage an existing customer to buy more, the accounts department is pummelling them for payment of an outstanding invoice.

There are ten fundamental reasons why we are where we are, all of which have the common thread of a need for leadership: of people, of focus, and of a cause (trust, ethics and as a global force for good).

1 *Outside in*
  There has been a focus on change from outside-in, not inside-out. It has been about change happening to people, not by people; about applying external processes rather than releasing internal passions. Many organizations have had the belief that someone outside of the organization has more good ideas than the people working within, and that is simply not true. As an organization, your next big idea lies within, not without. This outside-in approach, encouraged both consciously and unconsciously by too many consultants, has led to a culture of external reliance and dependence.

2 *Why are you here – what is your cause?*
  When organizations do not feel in control of their own destiny, especially in tough economic times, they focus on survival and internal operations, at the expense of their big picture, dreams

and cause. When organizations first start, they are clear on why they are starting. As they grow, and day-to-day operations take over the agenda, the big vision starts to disappear. I frequently ask Boards and senior leaders to write down what their organization stands for. I have never had two people agree and, more worryingly, almost all the contributions focus on internal, rather than external thinking and agendas.

3 *Ah yes, people. I remember …*
If an organization's perception in the world (read 'customers' and 'potential customers') is low, people in that organization feel low, and they are not valued as they could be, as an organization's number one, some would say only, asset. Organizations do not change, only people do, and it is the reawakening of people's energy, talent, ideas, gifts and potential that will play a massive part in being a next business great, especially in difficult times. Senior business leaders talk a good story about leaders being everywhere in their organization, but few do very much about it. Terms like 'empowerment' have not helped – it is not possible to 'empower' another human being; they are already empowered. The last 15 years have implied that senior people in an organization have some kind of hold over other people, which is again simply not true. Real, cultural (read 'people') transformation, reflected in openness, communication with no fear, and unleashed ideas and opinions, has not happened, and this has combined with financial uncertainties to make people focus more on their pension than their passion.

4 *Strategy and initiatives separated from day-to-day operations*
Few people get really passionate about Business Process Reengineering, or Total Quality Management, or Competency Based Frameworks. Such initiatives have too often been seen as being separate from day-to-day operations. Some, such as 'Right First Time', tried to be different, and actually led to inaction everywhere, with people being too scared to take risks or decisions in case things went wrong.

5 *The power of nightmares*
And so, over time, we become obsessed with what we are doing wrong, or worse, what we might do wrong anytime soon. This has led to a focus on what is 'wrong' with us as employees and as organizations, rather than what we do well. The only two

drivers for human beings are fear and pleasure. When we focus on the former, we look at protecting what we have, or not losing more; we create the fear agenda. This has led to a surge in 'risk management' by companies, many of which couldn't take a risk if their lives depended on it.

6 *We automatically move in the direction of our most dominant thoughts*

Many initiatives have focused on process, and not people and, furthermore, on increasing our knowledge about process. Such data/knowledge by itself is totally useless, and more of it only increases the jargon, hype and mystery about what is going on. We have enough information, thank you very much, and we have done a lot of analysis – analysing anything that moves, and quite a lot that doesn't. As a result, organizations become very complex, as initiative is piled onto initiative, and organizational structures are more to do with control than clarity. These have led to duplicated work, teams at war with each other, and an over-all lack of focus on releasing ideas, passion and true customer value.

7 *'I never knew such service was possible'*

Poor customer service is often the cause of decisions being made well away from the frontline. Decision-making is too often held in senior positions away from customers.

So, at best, when all is well, additional opportunities are not seized on (if a customer comes into your shop to buy a dress, and they buy a dress, that is not a sale, it is a transaction. It only becomes a 'sale' if they buy the dress and something else).

And, at worst, when things go wrong, your frontline people cannot do anything about it – and you lose not one customer, you lose many, as your ex-customers' tales of woe spread like wildfire.

The main reasons for these situations are a lack of frontline decision-making authority, and exposing an organization's internal processes and procedures to customers, rather than ensuring organizations have frontline decision makers.

8 *Do as we say, not as we do*

Talked, and not acted. Most decision-making has remained in the boardroom. And the boardroom is still too much the domain of well-educated, connected, middle-class white males. Many organizations do not reflect the cultural diversity of their customers, let alone their geography, and the male/female divide has been appalling, in particular when it is female skills that are now top of the must-have agenda for business leaders – empathy, communication, and personality.

9 *Softer skills just got real*

The recruitment of people has too often been done on the basis of technical skills and ability to do a particular role, rather than on the personality of the person. Yet, when we part company with people, it is almost always on the basis of personality, or behaviour. This has had the additional effect of suppressing people's true opinions and 'selves', which has led to a separation between people at home and at work, when of course we are always one and the same, wherever we are (even if, like me, your background is in IT).

10 *Information Technology has delivered a lot more …*

Information, and technology. However it has not delivered perceived value. My background is in Information Technology, so this one is very close to my heart.

On the one hand, technology has revolutionized our lives; the way we do business, how we communicate and deliver major advances in our health and education systems. On the other hand, over the last five years I have asked over 10,000 people, from companies from all over the world, the proportion out of 10 of IT projects that 'fail' to deliver (defined as late, over budget, or not meeting the needs of an organization). The lowest figure I have ever had is 9 (the latest official figure for the UK is 9.6).

Sadly, it is not entirely to do with perception. Chief Executives now know they can lose their jobs because of an IT project failing.

Which of these ten is holding your organization back? Write them down, with one action you will be taking to overcome them.

Journey Four – Be a Truly Authentic Organization

THE NEXT BUSINESS AGE – AN AGENDA OF HOPE

There has to be a better way, a way of ensuring our future is different from our past. And I believe there is, if we accept the premise that everything you need, to be anything you want, is already within you, and waiting. It is inside the hearts, minds and spirit of your people. It is time for all organizations, in all economic situations, to restore the power of hope, dreams and ambition.

We can, and must, move beyond 'the information age'. The 'knowledge economy' has not served us well, and has not delivered real, sustainable value for our stakeholders, our companies, our people and our world. We have plenty of knowledge, data and information, far more than we know what to do with. And by itself knowledge is nothing – our success comes down to:

- Whether we choose to do anything with it
- What we choose to do with it
- Why we choose to do what we do

At its very heart lie the natural gifts, talent and potential you and your people already have. If we want the future to be different from the past, we have to do different things, think in a different way, and be different. The next big thing is people … our challenge is that people are waiting for the next big thing. We must wait no more.

Welcome to the Next Business Age – The Leadership Economy, when we awaken the leaders within, unlocking the natural talent in your people, teams and organization.

Many people will tell you that you have something missing, to be more than what you have become. Many others will teach you that their answers alone will make you the very best that you can be. I now invite you to take a different perspective, yours, and to be the very best, that you already are.

People and passion over process and procedure – the choice programme

It is time to reinvent our organizations, awaken the leaders within, and take control of our own future, before someone else does. To be a business great, we must put:

- Cause over cash
- Clarity over confusion
- Choice over change
- Customers over convenience

Cause over cash

(Irony – organizations will make more cash as a result. And that is great – organizations must reduce costs and increase income)

- We are not only a great company; we are also a good company. Trust, ethics and integrity in all things and at all times – with corporate, social and world responsibility at the heart of all agendas. Your future success, and existence, depends on this. Making money and increasing income, while reducing costs, has to be central to everyone's agenda – combine it with a cause and your only source of income, your customers, will be proud to be your customers.
- Business has a powerful role, and responsibility, to transform our world and help our future generations inherit an earth of mutual respect, enlightenment and peace. To achieve this, business must change its drivers, so that instead of success being seen as

rewards for a few, it is measured on the positive impact it has for the many. Making money and profits can be complementary to this.

■ Everyone inside an organization knows their role in helping make the dream come true, and feels a part of that dream. Making money and profits can be complementary to this.

Clarity over confusion

■ Strip away the hype, the jargon and mystery surrounding your organization.

■ Deliver radical simplicity – clear, concise and compelling actions and futures.

■ Reduce red tape and processes, and agree an agenda in which every team, project and activity directly relates to you achieving your dream, vision, or whatever word you choose.

■

When I was at the Ford Motor Company, they always seemed to spawn the most inspired and motivated people. Completely passionate about what they did and the personal identity they associated with the corporate brand and aims. For example, if you ever meet a Ford employee ask them what they do career-wise; they will always reply, without hesitation: 'I work for Ford!' Never, 'I'm in HR', 'I'm a sales and marketing professional', 'I'm a software engineer', etc. Though what really differentiated these people is that they all had their own vision and made things happen, were incredibly bright, never seemed to get phased by anything, were incurably honest and self-critical, and always strived for team achievement.

Roy Sharples

■

Choice over change

(Irony – organizations will at last deliver the changes they have always wanted)

■ Organizations don't change; only people do, and no one has any true hold over anyone else. The paradox is that the only way to 'control' your people is to set them free. It is time to choose from within, not change from without.

■ Don't change for the sake of it – and above all, don't change what has worked in the past. For example, your organization may have and hold dear certain values. If you are a new leader, acknowledge what the organization has done well, and don't think you will be measured by how many changes you can make in the shortest possible time – people will see through this, every time.

■ There are no answers anymore. Best practice doesn't work, because what works in one organization may not work in another. So it comes down to the choices we make.

Customers over convenience

■ Your customers are why you exist. Without them, you have no business, or organization. They must be top of your priorities, in the eyes, minds and actions of all of your people. Your number one aim is to attract, retain and delight your customers.

■ Ensure your organizational processes, charts and roles reflect this. If your structure is vertical, put customers at the top. If it is horizontal, put customers end to end.

■ Put decision-making power where it belongs – with the people serving your customers. If you are a global organization (and if you have a website, then you are), allow for local services to adapt according to different cultures and customer needs.

Action

No space to write more lists – deliberately so. Just one question – what are you going to do to transform your organization?

Journey Four – Be a Truly Authentic Organization

TEN CHALLENGES, A THOUSAND CHOICES

And so to the 'how-to's …

I have my own ideas on how we can resolve the ten challenges listed; you will have your own. Indeed, for each one, there are thousands of different ideas and so-called 'solutions'.

This is the great irony for me: that there are so many choices, and yet, so often, we do exactly the same as we have always done. Is this madness? In seeking a different result, we have gone out and done what we have always done, and we are then surprised when we get what we have always got. So, the 'what' on those ten, with choices of action you can take to begin to make them happen:

1   Reinvent your organization from the inside out

So many people have spent so much time on 'organizational change'. This is always a waste of energy, money and time, because an organization cannot ever change; only its people can. This is the main reason that IT projects fail: not because the software does not 'work', but because of the people-changes that the software needs, in order to work.

What is your organization if not your people? What is your organization if not you? As it is people that change, and not organizations, they have to be our core focus. And those people will only ever change, or indeed do anything to the best of their abilities, for one reason, and one reason alone: because they want to. And they will make that decision based on their emotions, how they feel, and depending on what's in it for them. Unstoppable organizations realize that truly lasting change only happens through their own people.

Choices and ideas ...

- Replace change programmes with choice programmes.
- Ask each person in your organization for up to three specific ideas that would transform the company. Ensure a culture where imaginations and innovation thrive.
- Every single key supplier/consultant must transfer their key skills and knowledge to enable you to do what they do. Their number one aim must be to disappear, and their focus on the state you are in after they leave.
- Retain and grow what has worked in the past.

2 Have a relentless cause – a reason for being

And never compromise on it; make it crystal clear that this is why you exist. And focus on your core constituents, those who believe in your cause. You will always have differences of opinion on 'how' to achieve it; never compromise on the 'what'.

Choices and ideas ...

- Advertise your cause to attract the right people like a magnet.
- Be evangelical about your cause, and what it means for you, society, and the world.
- Everything you do, 100%, must ultimately focus on whether it helps bring your cause closer.

■

Why are we in business? For us it is not as simple as to make a profit. Like any company we require a profit to stay in business. But it is not the reason we are in business. The thing that has not changed from day one is the desire to make people think about the world we live in. This is, and always will be, why we are in business.

Howies
www.howies.co.uk

▪

Business is a powerful engine for social progress through the way it recruits and trains people, the way it produces, sells and disposes of products, the way it manages its impact on the environment, and the way it invests in the communities where it operates.

Business in The Community
www.bitc.org.uk

▪

For more on being a truly global, ethical organization, going way beyond corporate and social responsibility, please go to the website: www.nakedleader.com/forcesforgood.

3   Leadership – at last, its time has come

Place leadership at the very heart of your organization, in all that you do, and make it your number one priority to awaken the natural gifts, energy and potential of all of your people. Everyone has value. Welcome and value our differences, while ensuring people play their part through openness, trust and liberation. Control your people, by setting them free.

Choices and ideas …

- Hold genuinely open forums.
- Appoint a Leadership Director to the Board. This is absolutely critical to your success.
- You only need one supplier for leadership training and development – yourselves.

(And a fourth on this one – confront the 'negs': those people who disagree with everything you do, behind your back.)

If you think leadership is not important, please don't tell Ajmail and Sudarghara Dusanj. When they bought Cains it was threatened with closure, and Liverpool would have lost its only major commercial brewery. Through clear values, absolute self-belief and some tough, honest and open business decisions, they have turned it round. This in the cut-throat world of retail, with hard bargains driven by all. And the beer tastes very nice as well.

www.cainsbeer.com

4 Strategy and initiatives separated from day-to-day operations

Following on from 'cause' above, ensure your strategy becomes a 'how-to-achieve-it', and make it live and breathe in the eyes, experiences and lives of everyone. Relate all of your initiatives to the cause, and to ensuring that each has real, bottom-line value and measurable benefit. This ensures you will not be overrun with initiatives, and that people will not suddenly find themselves doing two jobs: the day job plus some randomly selected new idea. Revisit and review all of your initiatives. Do they help your cause? If not, ditch them.

Choices and ideas …

- Ensure every project has a clear value.
- Link your overall strategy with each of your departmental strategies.
- Make certain everyone knows the impact they are having on the overall big picture.

5 Focus on what you want, not on what you don't want

What do you do well? What do your people do well? Celebrate your successes, and map out how they happened so they become repeatable and sustainable. Keep the vision, dream, cause – whatever word works for you – uppermost in your mind, and make true decisions each and every day, at each and every meeting (a true decision is one in which you decide what you want, and you close off all other possibilities).

Choices and ideas …

- Reward people through specific and personal praise. As a leader or manager, take the blame for everything that goes wrong, while ensuring your people always take the praise for all that goes well.
- At the start of project meetings, ask people what is fantastic about this project, what the results will be for the company and your customers, and keep these thoughts uppermost in your mind – and form your project teams based on people's strengths (skill teams).
- In times of crisis, ask a different question. Instead of: 'Who's to blame?' ask: 'How does this event help us achieve our objective on time?'

■

Landmark knows what their members – small independent shops, wholesalers and cash-and-carrys – really want. In the retail world of 'biggest survives', they enable the small player and the individual entrepreneur to have new influence and bargaining power within the industry. Like every company I mention in this book, I admire Landmark for their belief, their collaboration and their optimism.

www.landmarkcashandcarry.co.uk

■

6   *People and passion over process and procedure*

All of your internal procedures must serve a purpose – that of your company and, therefore, your customers. We must remove our obsession with internal processes, and constantly ensure they serve our purpose, and not a software supplier or a consultancy. At the heart of your organization, place ownership, and a culture that it is not only

OK to belong to more than one team, but also that it is imperative you do. And, critically, that there are no right or wrong ways to structure your organization *vis-à-vis* centralized or decentralized. Achieve the best balance for your customers and costs, and run with it. This is an area I have seen businesses spend or waste billions on, as one year they bring everything into Head Office, and a few years later it's back out again, and so on.

Choices and ideas …

- ▪ Ensure your frontline people have the freedom to intervene and override processes that may not be working.
- ▪ For every process, ask yourselves 'So what?'
- ▪ Process software works only if you install it alongside a leadership/cultural transformation programme. If your people decide a system will not work, it won't.

▪

Many predicted that few would make purchases over the phone, or online. There wouldn't be the key elements of trust, personal contact or experience. Several companies have disproved this, by putting people over process.

Ebay's success is down to the trust created between complete strangers who will never meet. Amazon have transformed the entire book industry as the biggest library in the world with a no-questions returns policy, and First Direct have been the pioneers in 'faceless' banking – their customers love them. If these companies can put passion at their heart without personal contact, what can yours do?

▪

7   Delight your customer – make them want to buy

Do your customers love you? Do your customers sing your praises from the rooftops? Once you have released the awesome potential of your people, focus that new power on serving, delighting, gobsmacking your customers, every day, in all that you do.

Choices and ideas ...

- Know your customers better than they know themselves, particularly online. Segment your customers into your own (not an industry's) buying types.
- Yes, have a loyalty card; but you will learn so much more from customers who buy from you without needing a card. And, card or no card, make it very, very easy for your customers and potential customers to buy from you.
- In an age of technology and push-button services, put real people at your frontline, and make sure they have the real power to make decisions, i.e. whatever decisions your customers need them to be able to make.

(And a fourth. Every customer purchase – that's *every* customer purchase – is an emotional decision. And they get very, very emotional when things go wrong. This is a great opportunity to make them love you. However, you only have a few critical minutes, sometimes seconds, to make it happen. This is where, and when, you need your very, very best people.)

■

The Shaftesbury Group owns Covent Garden, and other prestige areas of London, on behalf of its institutional investors. When those shareholders, and their customers, visit Shaftesbury, they do not sit in a closed room listening to presentations and perusing spreadsheets: they go and see the sites they have invested in, meeting the people. Jonathan Lane, CEO, and his team, understand the passion of sharing an experience, rather than showing bits of paper. What can you do in your organization to make people's visits more exciting?

■

8   Do as we say, as we do, and as we are

Ensure that your organization reflects the cultural diversity of your society, and most certainly your customer base. Not because you want to be politically correct or look after minorities, but because you want to, because it is the morally right thing to do, and because it is commercially a very good idea! And check out your male/female numbers where they really count: on the board, in key positions around your company and, most importantly, at the frontline.

Choices and ideas …

- A board of three or more must have at least one female, selected on ability. If you have to appoint just because she is female, you have some serious work to do on leadership (this is the only time in this whole document the word *must* has been used)!
- Ensure you have different spokespeople for different situations.
- Country and cultural differences play a big part here. If you are international, or travel abroad, respect and understand cultural differences.

9   We are the same people, 24 hours a day

We are all living, breathing, emotionally-charged human beings. We do not have a work/life balance, because work is part of our life, and we do bring our lives to work. If you can reverse the culture of 'work,' or 'soon be the weekend', etc., you have indeed transformed your culture. Why can our workplaces and companies not be fun, fulfilling places of energy and excitement? Yes, of course we work to live, but we can also live to work.

Choices and ideas …

- Appoint a Leadership Director.
- Be flexible with your people (your number one asset) on working hours and ensure they can work at home as easily as at work (they will put in the hours at home if you trust them).
- Ensure people have time during the day to chat, and allow them to surf the net within the obvious general guidance.

10 IT's time to deliver

OK – we could write a book on this one. The IT industry has become the last great manual industry of our time. This does not have to be the case. IT projects are like every other project: they must be clear in goals, concise in explanation, compelling to do, and relate to the bottom line, to your cause. Strip away the hype, jargon and mystery surrounding IT.

Choices and ideas …

- Appoint an Operations Director to the board with the approach and characteristics on page 194 – this is absolutely critical to your success.
- There is no such thing as an IT project; everything is a business/ organizational project.
- If anyone internally or externally uses a term you think someone will not understand, ask them what it means, and do not apologize for asking.

Journey Four – Be a Truly Authentic Organization

THE PERSPECTIVES

People (employees and contractors)

To be the employer of choice

As a Next Business Great, your people will say things like:

- 'This is a great place to work – I love getting up in the morning.'
- 'The culture is open, I feel valued, my skills and talents are used every day.'
- 'There is no blame culture – no one says anything behind other people's backs that they would not be prepared to say to their face.'
- 'I feel a sense of belonging here – it is like my own company.'
- 'I feel valued – and in turn I offer constructive comments and ideas every day.'
- 'I am very well led, by people whom I respect and admire, and who say what they do, and do what they say.'
- 'I know whom I can go to, to ask any question, without fear or favour.'
- 'I am proud to be part of this company, and can hold my head up with my friends and family.'
- 'I bring myself to work every day, and give my very best because I choose to.'

- 'I can see how the work I do relates to the overall cause/strategy of the company, because I do not have a job specification: I have a person specification, an ongoing CV.'
- 'During tough times, decisions are made fairly and honestly, with tough decisions not hiding behind some fancy initiative.'

A Next Business Great: **CEO and Board**

To be the board of choice

We are aware of our power, our role, and our responsibilities to our people, to our customers, to each other and to the world. The buck stops here. To this end, we have clear roles, while encouraging each other to share our ideas and thoughts on any subject.

We are members of this board first, and representative of our functions second. We are all business people, and as such we all contribute openly to every topic discussed. We never (that is *never*) say anything behind each other's backs that we would not say to each other's faces.

Focus and agenda

The board of a Next Business Great only focuses on four activities:

Reputation
What you stand for, your cause, and how you are doing as a force for good in the world, and in the eyes of the world. Everyone is the Reputation and Cause Director. The global reputation of your organization, what people think of you, is the number one priority for truly authentic organizations in the 21st century. This includes going beyond corporate and social responsibility to being a truly ethical organization, as decided by your customers, employees and other stakeholders.

The Future
Your dreams and vision. Involve your people with their ideas, yes; however, ultimately they will look to you for leadership in this. This is the 'what' you are going to do, or 'where' you are going to be.

Don't get too hung up on whether your strategy has to fit a particular timescale; rather do it the other way around: what timescale best fits your strategy? It may be a year, five years, or in your lifetime.

Unleashing your talent within

The release of the potential, passion and personalities within your organization at every level. You need their ideas, their loyalty, and their energy, with particular emphasis on people dealing directly with customers and potential customers, on rising stars, and on your immediate successors – ensuring that you, as a board member, are absolutely dispensable.

Money

Relating everything back to finance. Without 'profit' – defined here as having more money coming in than going out (whatever you choose to do with that money) – you will cease to trade. This applies to everyone – entrepreneurs, health services, charities, sports clubs and governments.

▪

> Annual income twenty pounds, annual expenditure nineteen pounds nineteen and six pence, result happiness. Annual income twenty pounds, annual expenditure twenty pounds ought and six pence, result misery.
>
> ▪
>
> *Charles Dickens,* David Copperfield

▪

Unleashing the talent within your people must all be measured in financial terms.

Also, in all of these, freedom from external dependence is absolutely critical. Of course work with different partners, but those outside companies' number one priority must be to help set you free, and be self-sufficient. There will, of course, be some areas in which you need help (such as auditing). However, to be a Next Business Great means taking absolute control of your own destiny, and realizing that everything you really need to achieve it lies within you, and is waiting.

This is the ultimate in corporate governance – running your company properly does not mean relying on outside consultants at every turn. And every board member is responsible for all of these. It is no good wanting to be a Next Business Great, a truly outstanding organization, only to have everyone look at the Human Resources Director every time people are mentioned. You are all responsible for all of the above. End of story.

The Chief Executive Officer or Managing Director

Three key skills: presence, decision-maker, facilitator.

- The buck stops here – the ultimate arbiter.
- Facilitator at meetings, ensuring open and active contribution by all with balance of personalities.
- The company figurehead. The media love people and personality, not company brands or products – proactive in this area.
- In role for maximum three years, successor identified and all aware.

The Finance Director

Three key skills: business without jargon, building relationships, humility.

- Builds trusted relationships with key financial stakeholders, internal and external, e.g. stock market.
- Ensures compliance and proper conduct, with an independent third party overseeing this to ensure no conflict of interest.
- Focuses as much on dreams and opportunities as on cost savings.
- Speaks with no hype, jargon or mystery, and appreciates that finance is really as simple or as complex as we make it. Recognizes every other board member as a business person first and foremost, and is frequently asked and challenged on financial issues.

The Customer Director

Three key skills: influence and relationships; seeing different perspectives; global visionary.

■ Encompasses both sales and marketing, as neither of them happen, or work, without a customer.

■ Focuses on delighting existing customers so they love the company, and on attracting new customers. (Sounds simple? It is: put your best people in front of your customers.)

■ Ensures that everything the company does is focused on the customer, and that these customers are external, not internal (i.e. real customers).

■ Sees the world as a customer, so makes certain that the company is a force for good.

Note: the Customer Director is a combination of Sales and Marketing Directors. Think also about combining Sales and Marketing departments as well. The challenge with those titles is that they give too much of an internal focus, while everyone debates the boundaries and who is more important, when neither is as important as your customer.

The Leadership Director

Three key skills: humility, unbreakable self-confidence; outstanding communicator.

■ Facilitates the release of the natural potential of your people at all levels.

■ Ensures you only have one supplier in leadership – yourselves– and that every other partner works to this aim. Never outsource leadership.

■ Has in place internal coaching and mentoring, along with a clear structure of leadership academies and Master Classes.

■ Relates everything around human potential to real, measurable, bottom line figures and benefit.

Note: the Leadership Director is the new name for the HR Director. New name, new focus.

The Operations Director

Three key skills: agile and fast-moving – delivers projects in days not weeks, business and financially aware, leader of leaders.

- Ensures that all operations work smoothly around the needs and demands of your customers – end to end, horizontally across the organization.
- Responsible for what technology does, not what it is, as well as how it can transform the company and customer experience.
- Speaks in business English at all times, and commands respect as a business person at all levels in the organization.
- Influences perception of what is happening. Never refers to Service Level Agreements or utters the words 'user' (only one other industry has this term – the drugs industry!) or 'the business' – you are the business.
- Runs projects as a profit centre: every activity must be a business project and you must take on the role of ensuring benefits are delivered (in conjunction of course with the relevant functional owner).

Note: the Operations Director is a combination of a Chief Operating Officer and a Chief Information Officer or IT Director.

The Non-Executive Director

Three key skills: seeing the global picture, independent, dedication.

- Brings a genuine external/independent perspective.
- Spreads the positive word about the organization, each and every day.
- Knows where to go to find help when it is needed.
- Shares the same corporate responsibilities as Executive Directors during their tenure (maximum two years, ideally one).

Our values

- Trust, ethics and integrity are our highest values as a team. We place corporate and social responsibility at the very top of our agenda, and it is our stated aim to be a force for good in this world.
- Our cause is clear, and this is backed up by everything we do, and all that we are. Our point of view is also clear, concise and compelling.
- Leadership and brilliant ideas are not the exclusive domain of this board. Our role is to awaken leaders throughout our organization.
- As board leaders, we have in place our successors, and they know who they are.
- We value and seek to encourage open and different opinions in our team, and we all have equal value.
- When times are tough, we ensure decisions and communications are based on honesty, trust and integrity.
- Our board meetings are focused, we only make true decisions and outside the boardroom we are as one on all decisions made.
- We align our personal ambitions and agendas with those of our company, and we respect and value each other at all times.
- We are a global organization, no matter what our size or agenda – the Internet has made us that. We are a force for good in that world, in performance and perception.

A member of society

You are an organization I admire, because …

- You have placed your reputation as a force for good, as your number one priority.
- You have connected with other organizations that think and feel as you do, and have formed powerful alliances that help our world, by helping each other, in particular, those less fortunate than yourselves.

- You have partnered with local education and community groups, financing with money and/or time to help children and young adults – our next generation.
- You don't just talk about being such a force for good; you actually do something about it, and are always consistent with your beliefs and principles, in everything that you do. I expect there are many actions you are taking that I am not aware of.
- I may not be your employee, I may not be your customer, I may never transact with you in my life, I just want you to know that I admire and respect you, and all that you stand for.

Customers

To be my supplier of choice

- I am your customer, and I expect to be treated as such, and valued at all times.
- I know I am not always right. However when things go 'wrong' from my point of view, I expect to be listened to, respected, and cared for until it is put right. Of course, put it more than right, i.e. kiss me when I am hurt, and I will love you, and tell everyone I know about my experience.
- Your internal processes and procedures, fascinating though they may be, do not interest or excite me. So please don't tell me you cannot do something because of them: I won't believe you and I will get very bored. Just be honest and say that the way you do things around here is more important than me, and I will go elsewhere.
- The person I am with is you as a company, be it on the phone, a receptionist, or whoever. Don't invest billions in branding and then ruin it for me at the reception desk.
- I hate to be sold to, yet I love to buy. Calling people at home during family time may win you a few new customers, but it will upset even more.
- I prefer speaking with a person rather than a machine, every time.
- If I call you once with new information about me, I expect you to listen and make the changes needed. I will be frustrated if I have to keep repeating myself.

- I like every opportunity to help you to run your business better, and often I do know best.
- While I do not believe everything I read in the papers, there is no smoke without fire, so I will be watching very closely all that you do – in particular if you reward failure through large pay-offs for your Chief Executive.
- Your reputation as a force for good in this world is very important to me.

Shareholders

You are my investment of choice

I expect you to provide me with:

- Clear and concise information on how you are doing – both good and bad news;
- An opportunity to have a say in how you run your company, and to be listened to, and have my point of view respected;
- Evidence that you are a business force for good in the world in all that you do (this is a commercial necessity in the 21st century); and
- A healthy financial return, i.e. more money back than I invested.

I do not expect you to:

- Reward failure by your Chief Executive or other board members with huge pay-offs.

Competitors

You are a company I respect

You are a serious player in this market, who clearly values your people and your customers. We respect that, and we also note that you never, ever run down or attack us, in public, in advertising or in any other way. We may be competitors, but we can always respect each other and by doing so we can grow the overall market, benefiting both, and all, of us.

Do it!

Truly transform your organization (at last)

And so to the biggest question of them all.

Given that this leadership thing is very well documented – there are thousands of books and courses and events, with millions of words, ideas and actions out there … given that success is open and available to all – there are thousands of people who achieve amazing things for themselves and for other people, often from a very disadvantaged start …

Why?

Why is it that so many people, and organizations, never do it?

That is the ten million (any currency) question. Answer that one, and we overcome the final, biggest barrier of them all. This question has been with me ever since I first started my academic research (on Google), every day when I read another personal or professional development book and, especially, every time someone comes up to me and tells me:

- 'Your books are simply common sense.'
- 'The Naked Leader is the bleedin' obvious.'

Here are some things I've noticed, learned and experienced. Here are a few thousand of them – with no hype, jargon or mystery. Those you agree with, put into action. Those you don't agree with, put into action anyway – or do the complete opposite. Just, please, do something.

So, that massive question – why is it that so many people, and organizations, never do it?

- Is it because organizations don't know *what* to change?
- Is it because organizations don't know *when* to change?
- Is it because organizations don't know *how* to change?
- No, it is because organizations cannot change; only people can.

And so, whenever I have referred to 'organizations' or 'companies' or 'businesses' in this and my other books, all I mean is a collection of people who have happened to come together for a period of time, including you.

I believe there is one reason, and one reason alone, that organizations don't transform themselves: because they can't.

Organizations cannot change. Not now, not tomorrow, never in a million years. Organizations cannot change, because there is no such thing as an organization. Organizations simply do not exist, other than in the legal sense.

■

I was facilitating with the board of a well-known UK company. Eight leaders, who wanted to reinvent their organization. As soon as we had started we had a fascinating dialogue:

Chairman: 'The problem with this company … '
Me: 'You mean the problem with this team?'
Chairman: 'No, it's not this team.'
Me: 'Oh, I am sorry, you mean the problem with you?'
And we had an interesting chat.

Another example. A company with dual headquarters in London and New York were bringing together the top teams from both cities. They sat down on opposite sides of the room, and we had another fascinating example of ownership (not).

London: 'The problem with New York is … '
Me: 'You mean the city?'
London: 'No, I mean the New York team.'
Me: 'Oh, I am sorry, you mean these people here?' (I named them, one by one.)
London: 'No, not them, er, I mean … '
And we moved forward.

■

We do not move forward in our organizations, in my opinion, unless we realize one thing above all else. An organization can never reinvent itself; it can never change, it can never do anything – only its people can.

As leaders, how do we do this? By:

■ Winning over the minds, and hearts, of the majority of people.
■ Bravery.
■ Being the Leader of Choice.

Winning over the minds, and hearts, of the majority of people
When you share an idea, or a vision, your people fall into three camps:

- Some will be with you – they always are;
- Most will be unsure – these are your key people; and
- Some will be against you – they are against everything.

The key, absolute, and total focus must be on the first two groups, ensuring that as many people in the first win over as many people in the second. And you will never, ever do this through intellectual discussion, or logical persuasion. You will only ever do it by enabling those people to make the choice for themselves.

Go to www.nakedleader.com/negs for tips on how to handle the 'negs' in your team.

■

When *The Naked Leader* took off, I attracted a lot of praise, discussion, and some very, very unpleasant criticism. I decided to spend every Friday afternoon phoning people who were in this last camp. I had no real aim; I certainly did not want to 'convert' anyone. I suppose I simply wanted to say thanks for the email, I appreciate your thoughts, and have a great day.

It was fulfilling … at first. Then it became totally exhausting, and soon Friday afternoons became a nightmare. And then one day, I thought to myself, 'Why am I doing this?'

That said, there was one call I particularly enjoyed. I received this email (verbatim, name changed):

David
I have just given up on your appalling book, The Naked Leader.

The content was OK, although I've read better, but what an appalling way to structure a book. I got completely lost, and very, very angry. In the end I felt like a complete wa***er, being looked down on by a self-obsessed, anally retentive author.
Graham

And there, at the bottom, was a phone number. He had deleted his other contact details (I wonder why!) and he had left, sitting there all on its lonesome, his mobile number … I phoned him the next morning. He was on a train and had to shout. The conversation went like this:

'Hello Graham, it's David Taylor.'

'Who?'

'David Taylor.'

'WHO?'

'The self-obsessed, anally retentive author.'

'OH MY GOD – how did you get my number?'

'It was on the foot of your email.'

'I am SO sorry – and I loved your book, really.'

'No you didn't, and that doesn't matter – you got your feelings off your chest, I got to make this call, I really do not mind and I wish you well.'

'Er, same to you.'

And if you are reading this, Graham, I hope you like the structure of this one.

Bravery

When I arrived as a CEO at Software AG three years ago, there was a young man responsible for PR (Press Relations) and IR (Investor Relations). He was supposed to have been fired by my predecessor three or four times, but somehow he survived. I realized he was full of passion, but unfortunately PR and IR require distinct skills. IR requires a conservative, modest way of communication. PR is more aggressive. The sum of both created an average performance for both PR and IR. I advised him to focus, on IR – his more natural talent. I hired a PR manager and focused him on PR. The IR manager was disappointed. I began to empower him: full trust, full responsibility, stretched targets, full support and appreciation of his work ... This year we won two key IR awards, one being the No 1 IR department in the German stock index TecDAX. It was the result of ... empowerment, focus and trust, my principles of coaching.

Karl-Heinz Streibich
CEO, Software AG

■

Being brave means having absolute certainty – such a deep sense of belief in yourself, and in your team, and in the dream, that nothing, that is *nothing*, will stop you making it happen. Being brave also means recognizing, and unleashing, your team's leadership strengths, gifts and talents, and celebrating that many of them have skills that you do not have. It means playing politics – building powerful relationships.

Above all else though, it means being so certain of your own abilities, your own talents, and your own leadership, that you make yourself totally, and absolutely, dispensable, because you know that your true gifts lie within you, not in some role you happen to be carrying out at the moment.

That is not to say you do not put everything you can into your role. Indeed, quite the reverse; because you are absolutely certain of how amazing you are, you won't do what so many do – wait for permission, cover your tracks, plan for failure, stab others in the back.

The politics you play will be to build alliances, and trusted relationships. And it will be these that will help see you through. For example, if you are leading a major project, where are all the big decisions, the really tough ones, made? In project management meetings?

No way – they are a complete waste of time.

I will repeat that. Project management meetings are a complete waste of time. They are an excuse for people to cover their backs, to outshine each other, and to talk, talk, and talk some more. The big decisions happen between the one or two really key players on a project, players who have built up such trust and faith in each other that they will say anything, ask any question, and get straight to the point.

And by the way, have your successor identified early on – you are only passing through this role on your way to greatness.

A long business coaching story – cut short

The situation. We as a company did not feel we were being treated with any professional respect by our customers: we were being blamed for everything, we were always treated as lesser beings and now we were about to not be paid.

My second in command, Buddy, wanted to resolve this, but did not know if he was brave enough.

I could so easily have stepped in and made a decision, but that would be undermining. My decision would have been to threaten to up and leave the project (in Norway) and fly back to the States …

So I asked Buddy a series of business coaching questions like: 'What is the most important thing you need to get over this crisis and put the project back on a proper course?' and: 'What is the worst thing that can happen?' and finally: 'How can you catch their attention in a way that will push home the point on how serious we are about what needs to be done?'

To this last question, Buddy replied: 'We could threaten to send everyone home,' and his face went sheet-white. I replied: 'Great idea! This shows leadership and guts. I will back you to the hilt and take responsibility.'

We did this, they came to the table, the project was successful, and they admired us, and paid us!

Everyone on the project grew a little that day. Because of Buddy, not because of me.

John Maitz
VP FS EMEA
Computer Sciences Corporation

▪

Being the Leader of Choice

The personal approach to customer service is making a comeback – it is one of the most innovative initiatives of the 21st century.

▪

A girl told me at a school how she entered a phone-in competition that was on the Disney Channel. She had entered many. This one was different. When she called, instead of hearing a recorded voice saying press 5 then 7, etc., a man answered her call. She was completely thrown, gave her answer and then went running around the house yelling: 'I got a person!'

▪

Much has been covered in The Naked Leader books on leadership (I hope!). Overall, to me, to be the Leader of Choice in the 21st Century there are four key actions/behaviours above all others. They are to:

- Inspire others by your very presence – by what you say, do, and are. To do this, it will be the real leadership skills that matter. These are listening, the ability to build and retain rapport with anyone and everyone, and democratic toughness – seek information and opinions, but always know that, at the end of the day, the buck stops with you.
- Take the blame for everything, and praise others for everything – sincerely, specifically, and personally.
- Ensure that people love coming to work. I will repeat that. Ensure that people love coming to work. We do this by finding out their passions, their reasons for choosing to give their best, and we do all we can to meet and exceed those expectations (and money will rarely be the number one: people rarely give their best for money alone).
- Know that your fundamental task is the motivation of others, releasing that motivation into an unstoppable energy, and ensuring that energy is totally focused on achieving your collective dream.

Indeed, as a Leader of Choice, you know that it is in no one's interest for you not to display your gifts, whilst helping others display theirs.

What to do next

1 Compare the principles, ideas and vision in this blueprint, to what you want to do, or be – your ideal future of choice. Choose which parts of the blueprint to overlay on your own vision.
2 Compare the principles, ideas and vision in this blueprint, to where you are now.
3 Now have a 'reality' session, when you list all of the reasons, facts and risks, and most of all, how impossible it all is to achieve.
4 Now take true and total ownership – that being a Next Business Great, a truly outstanding organization, is not only within your choice, it is an imperative. Revisit all of the 'reasons' and label

them as 'excuses,' the 'facts' that are really only 'opinions', and then the 'risks' that are, of course, 'opportunities'. Finally, if your dreams really are 'impossible', why aim for anything less?

5   Focus on the business grails, delivering real, measurable and sustainable customer value and profit from:

- reputation, and corporate and social responsibility;
- the release of your people's potential, and ideas;
- information technology;
- teams; and
- projects.

6   Keep taking action, which will either take you closer to where you want to go, or who you want to be. If an action takes you closer, do more of the same; if it takes you further away, do something different, and if that doesn't work, go to 7 below.

7   Do something different, always measuring the results.

Journey Five

– Coaching the World

Journey Five – Coaching the World

LIFE'S MOST PERSISTENT QUESTION

Life's most persistent and urgent question is: what are you doing for others?

Martin Luther King

However you want to be remembered, I am sure there is one epitaph that will be high on your list. *You would want to be remembered for the good that you have done.*

Your autobiography will live forever, in people's minds, in what you leave behind, decided by what you do today. This is the first reason we would all want to help other people. The second is this: you will never achieve your dreams without the help of others, and your loved ones will never achieve theirs without yours.

This is a Journey you will be taking with other people – as you help them and as you teach them. You are teaching and coaching and mentoring other people, all of the time, with what you say, what you do, and how you are, each and every day. It's called communication, relationships, rapport, and politics. You do it all the time.

So when you ask yourselves should I coach my children or someone at work, please remember you are already doing this, all of the time. By what you say and what you do, which combine to make you who you are.

Sometimes we may say one thing and do another, and the message is mixed. If you smoke or swear, and you tell your child not to, which message wins through – what you do, or what you say? What you do, every time.

If I were to ask you whether you would help someone in real need, or if you would help a neighbour by giving them a lift to the shops, or if you are a force for good in the world, you would probably say yes to them all. Because words are easy.

If I were to ask you to go and find someone who needs your help right now, or ask around to identify a neighbour who needs that lift, or to take a stand for something you believe in, in the world, you would probably think twice. Because action takes time and effort.

How many of you know a manager at work who drones on and on (and on) about what a great leader they are, and how they know 'all this stuff' and yet they don't put it into practice, ever? They are coaching those around them, all the time. To be a talker, not a doer.

This Journey invites you to take action – to do something. It takes place in your life, as you live it, and will have a profound, positive influence on many people. And all you need, above anything else, is the right intention.

Claire Westwood shares a real experience on intention

I was facilitating a leadership event. Sitting at dinner with the delegates after the first day, one of them said to me: 'What you have shared with us today, Claire, is very, very powerful. In fact, it is so powerful, that we don't feel you should be telling people this stuff. Taking control of our thoughts, how to influence and persuade others, how to design destinies for ourselves and our organizations. What we feel is that if this stuff got into the wrong hands, it would be very dangerous. People would be manipulated and hurt.'

I asked him a question: 'In your kitchen at home, do you have knives?'

'Yes, of course,' he said.

'And how many people have you killed, or at least stabbed, with those knives?' I asked.

■

Intention. Everything I have shared with you in *The Naked Leader* books is in the public domain, and available to all. Perhaps not in this format, but it is there and has been for many years. And what you do with it, what you choose to do, and how you act, and behave, for yourself and for other people, is entirely your choice. If you intend to hurt and to harm, that is what will be the result. If you decide to help and to heal, that is what will happen. It is not what we know that matters; it is what we do with what we know.

Many people talk about 'random acts of kindness'; many books inspire us to carry these out and make a real difference in others' lives, every day. This Journey invites you to go beyond that – way beyond. From inspiration to transformation.

With inspiration, or motivation, people feel good about themselves, their dreams, and about what they are capable of. That is fantastic, yet it is not enough, because people who are inspired need to take action quickly, to show to themselves that the inspiration has achieved something for them, and that it works.

■

Inspiration is energy, a passion, and it has to be used – before it disappears.

■

And if it is not applied, it simply disappears, or becomes delusion. When we combine inspiration with action, we are less likely to go back, to return to our original thinking, actions, or even way of life. That is transformation.

To choose to change our lives needs inspiration; to choose to change our lives forever needs action. To make that change repeatable and embed it into our lives, we need to take a specific action. When we do this we move towards being transformed. And as with us, so with each other.

And so, as well as helping each other on this Journey, I invite you to coach them to help other people, to start a positive chain, a transformational virus of action and reaction.

You hold a great power in your life, as a facilitator, with one simple goal – to help others to be the very best that they already are. You will do this by:

- *Helping them to identify what is 'right' in their lives.* We are all continually bombarded with 'evidence' and opinion on what is wrong with us – at home from our partners and families, at work from our peers and our boss, and from the media about our world.

■ *Identifying their strengths – and celebrating these – while being gentle and affectionate about our/their weaknesses.* When you first explore this area, people may be humble about these. I facilitated a Master Class once where the first contributor said their main strength in life was their ability to do an excellent Excel spreadsheet! While not questioning this, I simply asked if there was anything else they would like to be remembered for.

And by avoiding:

1 *Judgements that anything about the person you are with is 'right' or 'wrong', in the sense of answers being correct or incorrect.* There simply is no correct way of achieving something – there are only actions that take you closer to what you want to be, or where you want to go ('helpful') and those that do not ('unhelpful'). The best way to avoid making judgements is to avoid issuing commands or making statements (that only leaves you with questions, by the way)!

2 *The twin traps of 'you are not enough' and 'how good can you be?'* The first tells people to be more than what they have become. This is the message of too many so-called leadership gurus, who imply that, because we have not achieved this or that in our lives, we have not achieved enough. The two greatest challenges here are first, it makes us regret, or somehow feel ashamed of something we have done in our past (which we cannot change now), and worse, it is the beginning of a message that tells us we would be better off by being someone else, rather than ourselves. This of course leads to the 'you've got something missing'. You have nothing missing. You can achieve anything you want, by simply being yourself. The second is more inspirational – inspiring people to be the very best that they can be. The trap here is that people can spend a lot of time working out how good they can be, and the whole exercise becomes an intellectual process, as we analyse how amazing we can be. Organizational strategy often falls into this trap. Instead of looking at what their customers love about what they are doing right now, and doing more of that, they spend time in workshops 'blue-skying' where they could go next. Nothing wrong with all of this; however, it doesn't often lead to fast action, and immediate results. When people ask

you for your help, or you offer to coach or guide someone, they may be vulnerable.

3   *The charisma of nurturance and dependency.* We have this as a boss or a parent. If you are in this position, remember you are starting from a position of power *over* someone, rather than *with* that person.

4   *The charisma of the ideal self.* Like, you have discovered something that others have not, and when they open their eyes, and do what you do, they may well make the same discovery! No!!! Avoid!!!!!

5   *A leader who determines good and evil – moral certainty.* You do not make up rules for other people. Most of us find it a challenge to live our lives in our own way, without imposing these thoughts, beliefs, opinions and often truth (the way we see things to be) – this dogma – on others.

And, just before we begin, a question you may have already asked: what's in it for you, in helping other people on this Journey? An important question, because there *has* to be something in it for *you*, or you won't do it.

▪

It is one of the beautiful compensations of life, that no man can sincerely help another without helping himself.
Ralph Waldo Emerson

▪

You will gain three main benefits from helping others in the big ways I suggest in this Journey:

▪   *You will change the world.* By helping just one other person, you change their world, for good. By asking them to help others, you change someone else's world, as well.

▪   *You change your world.* It feels great to help others – we feel a better and braver person – and why not?

▪   *What we sow, we reap.* Huge irony here – the more you give to others, the more you receive in return. If you want to *get-get-get*, then *give-give-give*.

You do not have a finite amount of love that will disappear when you give it out – you have unlimited love, warmth and generosity. Even if it were not replenished, returned to you tenfold, through your acts of help, you would still have plenty left over. Given that it is replenished, you will be overflowing with infinite energy, warmth and love.

There is one way, and one way only, to overcome this fear.

▪

I remember feeling very uncomfortable at one of my first events. I was sitting backstage with one of the other speakers, and she was reassuring me that I would be fine. Just before it was my time to go on she took my hand and said: 'Go out there and be your best.'

To which I replied: 'The trouble is, I don't feel like being my best.'

And she said: 'Then go out and be your best, anyway.'

And I did.

▪

Anyway. You are uncomfortable at the idea of doing something you have to do – do it, *anyway.* You are unsure about saying what you feel has to be said – say it, *anyway.* You are uncertain whether you can be your dream – be it, *anyway.*

And that is powerful: indeed, it is enough to make us take action, in itself. For many people this is enough.

However those feelings of doubt and uncertainty, and being uncomfortable, can come back very quickly. And therein the next hurdle – we decide to remove the feelings.

We now find ourselves in a paradox: we need to have those feelings of discomfort, as a spur to move us forward, yet if they take us over, we stand still. Add in all sorts of other emotions and we will very soon be in a state of paralysis. Unless we do something different; unless we do the opposite of what we have always done …

And you will be helping yourself, as well. Your self is just as important as other selves. On this Journey, I invite you to help your self, to help other people, and to encourage other people to help each other … through actions that will have a profound effect …

▪

All that is necessary for evil to thrive is for good people to do nothing.

▪

Yes, one has heard the above expression many times; the danger is when one ceases to be challenged by it.

▪

First they came for the Jews
and I did not speak out
because I was not a Jew.
Then they came for the Communists
and I did not speak out
because I was not a Communist.
Then they came for the Trade Unionists
and I did not speak out
because I was not a Trade Unionist.
Then they came for the Catholics
and I did not speak out
because I was a Protestant.
Then they came for me
and there was no one left
to speak out for me.

Pastor Martin Niemöller

▪

Journey Five – Coaching the World

THE 21 DAYS

I have allocated the tasks a colour according to their degree of bravery and impact – on yourself and the other person/people. Borrowed from the world of judo and in the spirit of Naked Leader, a white belt is a high degree of impact, green is massive and black is for bravery beyond description.

Plan 21 days over the next month, by deciding what you want, when …

Belt	Self	Someone close / partner	The next generation	Career	Stranger
White	Find magic every day	Surprise your partner	Give your most precious commodity	Play Naked Coach Career Bingo	Connect while driving
Green	Experience great customer service	Feel great power and humility	Help a child learn new and more helpful rules	Bring yourself to work	Reconnect with a friend
Black	Men – find closure All – coach your family!	Fall in love once again with a partner of many years	Connect with children, while helping them	Women – be successful by being yourself All – make yourself totally dispensable	Give time to an older person

Journey Five – Coaching the World

IT STARTS ...

For yourself

White belt: find magic every day by making the ordinary extraordinary ...

Every day we hypnotize ourselves to only see the ordinary. We live in homes we think we know so well, we travel on journeys that become all too familiar, and we meet the same type of people each and every day ... or do we?

All we have to do is look around – really look, and we see something new. Take a walk in your garden, feel the texture of a wall at home, look around you on that daily journey to work, and as you see someone, say a silent thank you to them for being unique – totally and absolutely unique ... just like everyone else.

In praise of cranes

I suppose I had never really noticed them before, or I'd taken them for granted. Yes, it must be the latter; after all they are rather tall, colourful and have flashing lights. Taken them for granted – yes, that's it – as we often do with what serves a purpose, rather than the purpose itself.

And then, one day, I was stopped in the street by a friend I was with.

'Look,' she said. 'Look up there,' and she was pointing at a huge, red crane and, more exactly, at the crane driver/operator.

'I couldn't do that,' she added, 'could you?'

'Wouldn't want to,' I gave a typical non-answer that avoided her question. And then I thought about the question. I looked up again, at the driver, at the crane, at the vertical ladder in the middle, at what the crane was doing. And I then gave a proper reply:

'No, I couldn't do that.'

And we just stood there, two adults staring at a piece of mechanical equipment as though through the eyes of a child. Finding beauty, wonder and amazement in something we had each seen many times, and had never really seen, least of all appreciated. Like the bird from which it takes its name, it was flying, and yet it was grounded. It was graceful as it lifted weights like no other, and soon, as I was to learn later, its base would be concreted into the final building/structure it had played such a part in creating.

How functional, my left brain thought.

How fitting, my right brain chipped in.

And how fleeting these moments when we can, if we so choose, stop and appreciate, and stare, and enjoy, in a completely new light.

Yes, a crane is there to serve a purpose, and how powerful that is, to help others achieve their dreams, quietly, easily, effortlessly.

I would never look at a crane in the same way again. Next time, I would really see.

From Jonathan, in Canada, by email

▪

Also, when we focus all of our attention – our sight, our hearing, our thoughts – on just one thing, one event, one activity, we can discover peace, wonder and magic – the unusual in the usual. Take washing the dishes. We dread the moment coming, our ego belittled, our creative self creating at the indignity of being dragged away from creation. And we run the water and we put in the liquid and we make a start – with a clatter and a bang. And we think about what we did today, and what our plans are for tomorrow. And then we might look down at the one, single plate we are washing, and we notice its colour, for the first time, and we feel its texture, and we focus all of our attention, mind, body and spirit, on this plate. And when we do the dishes, and only do the dishes, we open that biggest door of all, to inner peace, to oneness, and to true enlightenment.

The Seven Wonders of the World

A group of students were asked to list the 'Seven Wonders of the World'. Although there were some disagreements, the following received the most votes:

1   Egypt's Great Pyramids
2   Taj Mahal
3   Grand Canyon
4   Panama Canal
5   Empire State Building
6   St Peter's Basilica
7   China's Great Wall

While gathering the votes, the teacher noticed that one quiet student hadn't turned in her paper yet. So she asked the girl if she was having trouble with her list.

The girl replied: 'Yes, a little. I couldn't make up my mind because there are so many.' The teacher said, 'Well, tell us what you have, and maybe we can help.'

The girl hesitated, and then read: 'I think the Seven Wonders of the World are ... :

1   To see
2   To hear
3   To touch
4   To taste
5   To feel
6   To laugh
7   And to love.'

The room was so quiet you could have heard a pin drop. The things we overlook as being simple and ordinary, and that we take for granted, are truly wondrous.

Bob Armstrong

■

Green belt: experience great customer service …

… by noticing, and acknowledging, great customer service.

When we believe something to be true, we see the world in that way. And so with customer service. So, today, actively look out for amazing service. It may be in a shop, it may be inside your organization; it will happen at some stage, if you are looking for it, if you are expecting it. Because people usually rise to meet your highest expectations.

And if you want to encourage it, instead of being in your role as a customer (I am the customer here, your role is to serve me, because as your customer not only am I always right, I am greatly superior to you), change it to one of a meeting of two people in a single moment in life. Two human beings, one of whom happens to have a need, and the other who is meeting that need. And, as you meet, as two human beings, mentally send the other person total, absolute, unconditional warmth and love. Now, watch what happens.

◾

I was flying to Helsinki in Finland, with Finnair. I had some ideas for this book, and the only thing I could find to write on was the sickbag. What I wrote was very important to the book. For some reason I did not put the bag into my pocket, but back in the front of my seat. When I got off, I forgot all about it, until after I had spoken at the conference and was making my way back to my hotel.

I needn't have worried. Much to my surprise, when I checked in that evening, the receptionist handed me an envelope with my name on – and inside was the sickbag with my notes on.

Thank you , Finnair.

◾

And I can't begin to wonder how they did that …

That is an extreme example. Day-to-day, if you believe that customer service is generally poor, that is what you will find. Or … you know the opposite.

By the way, the personal approach to customer service is making a comeback – it is one of the most innovative initiatives of the 21st century. Check www.iwasgobsmacked.com for some amazing customer service experiences.

Black belt – for men: find closure

The main person we seek approval/permission from is our father or mother. However, this works equally well with sons or daughters:

How to make peace with your father

You have to do this before you can truly be the very best that you already are, and be at peace with yourself, which is what we all ultimately seek. This may involve swallowing your pride, putting your ego to one side, and/or great bravery. This is also the best 'researched' paper I have ever written – it works every time.

1   If your father is alive

Take ownership of the relationship. Many men complain about their father not spending time with them, many women say their father is/was too strict, both sexes often feel their father could have shown their love or pride far more. By taking owner-ship you reverse this – so that you take responsibility for what happens in the relationship now.

This alone is both powerful and challenging – and through *both of these* comes a feeling of peace.

Choose your moment. This has to be face-to-face and not made a 'big thing' of – in the course of a conversation about normal, day-to-day stuff, when you are together with no one else present, and when there is a pause, say the following:

'Dad, while we are together, I want to thank you.'

He will reply with something like 'What for?' or similar. Let him say whatever he says, as this will now involve him in the 'discussion'.

You then say: 'For ...' (then in your own words say some-thing general about his role in your upbringing, followed by something specific that he did, to illustrate) and then stop.

Remember, you only need one specific example – never forget your aim, to make peace.

Your father will give one of three reactions: he will be surprised or embarrassed or receptive, or he may be a mixture of all three. His most likely reaction will be to deny that he played such a big role, and he may express regret at things he could have done better.

Whatever his response, go to him, look him in the eyes and say: 'I just wanted to say thank you, and to say (either) I am very proud of you/I love you.'

Whatever his response, and it will most likely be positive, throw out unconditional love to him in your mind. Then, if you feel it is appropriate, hold each other – either cuddle or hold hands. And let feelings of peace, of love, and of calm flow through you as you enjoy the reconnection with the man who played such a big part in bringing you into this world or, in the case of a stepfather, who played a big role.

Be in the moment, be totally present. And then offer to make him a cup of tea, or something else that changes the situation.

2 If your father has passed away

Two possibilities. And please have an open mind as you read both, especially the first.

One – do the same *as if* he were alive, in your mind. Imagine the whole conversation, both ways, in real time, with your father 'sitting' opposite you. Remember our mind cannot tell the difference between something that happens in 'reality' and something it imagines with emotional intensity.

So, think as you would think; act as you would act; feel as you would feel.

Remember your aim here – it is to be at peace. So, in your mind, it will be real.

Two – Find somewhere quiet, relax and be at peace. Cover yourself mentally with a purple cloak or curtain, make it a very deep purple, large and sweeping, and let it flow all over you. Breathe, relax.

Now, allow people whom you have argued with, fallen out with, hurt, or been hurt by, to enter your mind, one by one. Perhaps start with a teacher from your school days. Acknowledge them as they come into your mind, and look at them for a few seconds. They are some distance away from you: it is like watching them on a cinema screen. Now, let them go, see them disappear from your mind forever, and as you do, say to yourself, out loud or simply in your head: 'I choose peace over this.'

Next, allow your father to enter your mind. Acknowledge him as he does so, and look at him for a few seconds. He is some distance away from you: it is like watching him on a cinema screen. He is smiling at you with love and joy, as if he really misses you. Now, watch as he steps out of the cinema screen and slowly walks towards you. He sits next to you, and you hold hands.

And as this happens, say to yourself, out loud or simply in your head: 'I choose peace, and I choose you.' Stay together for as long as you wish, and then let him go in peace, back onto the screen and then watch him walk away.

Finally, say to yourself with total love: 'I allow this moment to be as it is.' – slowly, three times.

My personal experience

For years I had complained that my father had managed my expectations when I was younger, had rarely, if ever, told me that he loved me, and never said he was 'proud' of me. And as this book unfolded, I realized that if I was going to be true to the words I was writing, and to find peace, I had to do something about it.

So, we met up in the Lake District for a walking weekend. My plan was to wait until the Sunday and, on a long walk, to ask him if he was proud of me.

We met on the Friday evening and went straight in to dinner. The restaurant was very full, and we chatted about family and walking and this book. My Dad and I have never been wine connoisseurs, and so we asked the waitress which wine she would recommend. She suggested a something or other, and added that it was 'number 42 on the list'.

And my Dad then spoke, to her, and said words that brought me instant peace. He said: 'Ah, number 42. That will mean a lot to my son, David. He finished his first book at chapter 42. It is brilliant. I am so proud of him.'

At which the waitress smiled politely, and walked away. At which tears welled up in my eyes, and I looked at my Dad, and told him that I loved him, too.

■

And yes, it works for mothers and daughters too, and all the variations!

After you have done this, have a laugh together. If nothing else, read him this:

■

An elderly man lived alone in a village. He wanted to dig over his potato garden, but it was very hard work. His only son, who would have helped him, was in prison. The old man wrote a letter to his son and mentioned his situation:

Dear Son,

I am feeling pretty bad because it looks like I won't be able to plant my potato patch this year. I hate to miss doing the garden, because your mother always loved planting time. I'm just getting too old to be digging up a garden plot. If you were here, all my troubles would be over. I know you would dig the plot for me, if you weren't in prison.

Love, Dad.

Shortly, the elderly man received this telegram:

'For Heaven's sake, Dad, don't dig up the garden!! That's where I buried the GUNS!!'

At 4 a.m. the next morning, a dozen armed agents and local police officers showed up and dug up the entire garden without finding any guns. Confused, the man wrote another note to his son telling him what happened, and asked him what to do next.

His son's reply was: 'Go ahead and plant your potatoes, Dad. It's the best I could do for you from here.'

With thanks to Robin Doherty

■

Black belt for all: coach your family to sing!

Imagine it's someone's 18th birthday. It's time to sing *Happy Birthday*, and with childhood bravery, adolescent cheek and adult politeness you are going to coach those around you into singing one of the most popular songs in the world.

So, all together now:

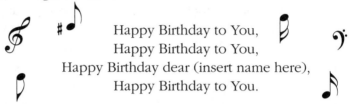

Happy Birthday to You,
Happy Birthday to You,
Happy Birthday dear (insert name here),
Happy Birthday to You.

And as they sing, how do they sing? This is perhaps the happiest song on the planet, ever. It is also the simplest to remember, and yet so many people sing it like they are at a funeral, head down, facing the flow, mumbling with embarrassment.

So, time to do some coaching. In a very friendly, warm and fun way …

Get everyone to sing it through once and then say that was fantastic, but we can make it even better, something that the birthday girl, or boy, will remember for the rest of their life.

Best check everyone knows the words (four lines repeated, with the only difference being swapping the 'you' with 'dear name' in the third line). A total of just six different words! Then ask people where the emphasis of the song is:

Is it:
HAPPY Birthday to You
Or
Happy BIRTHDAY to You
Or
Happy Birthday to YOU?

It's clearly the last – so, now invite everyone to sing the song with the emphasis on 'You'. They will start and it will sound something like this:

Happy Birthday to YOU
Happy Birthday to YOU

Stop them after two lines, and point out that the birthday person is in danger of having nightmares, and that this emphasis is more like a physical attack than a celebration. Also, now is a great time to remind everyone that this is a joyous, happy song, so if you are feeling such joy and good feelings when you are singing, it might be a good idea to tell your face.

Now, ask them to sing it again, and it will be much warmer. Again stop them after two lines, as there is one part still missing. Tell people that when we communicate, the power of our message is not in the words we use, but in our body language. Maybe we could hold our arms forward in a loving way, and lean forwards towards the person, even move into a circle and surround them as we sing.

Now, with all of those things together, sing it once more and just watch the reaction on the birthday boy or girl. The question is, of course, are you brave enough to do this at the next family gathering?

(That's why it's a *black* belt.)

For your partner

White belt: surprise your partner …

Sometimes the most powerful impact can come from the most simple of actions.

Men:

Say: 'I love you.' And mean it. And really mean it – like you did the very first time you ever said it. Like you will say the last time you ever say it – and that day will come.

Women:

Send your partner flowers. That's right, send flowers to a man. Not to embarrass him in public, rather to tell him that you love him, in private. And do it on just any day – not his birthday, not on your anniversary … on any other day when he is least expecting it. He may not have a clue what to do with them once they have arrived, indeed it may well be the first bunch of flowers he has ever received. Deep down, though, deep down, his pulse will race a little faster.

Green belt: feel great power and humility

By 'losing' an argument at home (or work). Do this by ensuring someone else has the last word. Do this by avoiding a bigger argument which you will only regret later, and which you don't have time for. And be genuine. Don't go for the simple option and 'lose' any old argument – give way, genuinely give way, on something that you have been stubborn about.

It will feel very (very) uncomfortable at first, and then make you feel very special. And do it more than once, and watch what happens. Also, watch the person whom you are 'losing' the argument with: you will actually be closer to them than if you had held out ...

Black belt: storybook reunion

> My husband and I have been married for 31 years. Last year we decided to separate. We had grown apart, and had become like strangers in the same house. All that we had previously loved about each other had disappeared, and each day became a bore and a grind. We decided to give each other a 'separation gift' and I gave him a copy of *The Naked Leader*.
>
> Two months after he read it, he gave it back to me with a note in it that said: 'If you leave me, can I come too?'
>
> That was last year. Last month ago we reaffirmed our marriage vows at our local church. We have fallen in love all over again. We have rediscovered our love, our friendship and each other. All that we had previously loved about each other has returned, and each day is full of magic. We have decided to become friends, and stay.
>
> *Extract from an email*

Life doesn't get much better than receiving an email like that. Of course, it had nothing to do with me. It was entirely their choice, and they chose to see each other afresh, to stop looking for what was 'wrong' in each other, and value what was 'right' about each other.

In a world where separation and divorce is becoming the norm, without taking a huge moral stance, I only ask you this – if things are not going well with your loved one, why don't you fall in love once again?

■

Acceptance and forgiveness

> When we accept that things/people are the way they are
> ... then there is nothing to Forgive!
> When we accept that what we said/did at the time needed to be expressed
> ... then there is nothing to Forgive!
> When we accept that what happened provided us with the best way to learn
> ... then there is nothing to Forgive!
> When we accept our own self as we are
> ... then there is nothing to Forgive!
> Acceptance is hard to learn – and more gentle to practise.
> Forgiveness links us into patterns of judgement all over again and makes it more difficult to move on.
> Of course it doesn't mean we just sit back, and if we can face ourselves in the mirror and can honestly accept that we did our best under the circumstances, with the information available at the time
> ... then there is nothing to Forgive!
>
> *Sharon Galliford*

■

For your next generation

White belt: give your most precious commodity

■

> Who am I being if my children's eyes are not smiling?
>
> *Ben Zander*

■

Which is not your *time*; it is your *self*.

We all talk about not having enough time to give to our children, or grandchildren, or to our nieces or nephews, and yet when that time does arrive, we are already too tired to play – and young people can always tell. They can always tell when they do not have your total and absolute attention focused on their favourite subject – themselves.

Your children would rather have ten minutes of *you*, than an hour of just your time. And this applies at mealtimes (and really listening to them), when watching TV (we watch TV with our young children and then stop doing so when they become teenagers – why?), and showing genuine interest in their music.

■

Having grandchildren is your reward for not killing your children when they were teenagers.

Bizarre proverb

■

And remember, any and every time you choose not to do this, you are not only making an excuse, you are placing something else as a higher priority. One day, your children will grow up, and that day will come sooner than you think.

As I have had the great fortune to travel around the world, I have discovered that football is the universal language. It brings together communities; it ignites hope and desperation in equal measure.

On Wednesday, 25 May 2005, Liverpool won the European Championship with the greatest comeback in football history, winning on penalties after extra time against AC Milan after being 3–0 down at half time. I write 'the greatest comeback in football history' as if it was a fact, not an opinion. It must be a 'fact' as I am a lifelong Evertonian. I salute Liverpool's achievement as both a classic example of belief, persistence, and being one team, and as a catalyst in this moving story of love between a father and his son.

■

My story, my life, my son

I left early that morning carrying his dream; his wise words resonating deep inside me: 'Never underestimate the power of your ability.' His dream was our dream. It had unlocked passion for him, and given him a sense of belonging. It had nurtured pride, it had unwrapped a rich tapestry of emotion, and it had exposed tears and brought joy.

'Make us dream' had been his evocative cry. And so we dreamt, and so much more.

Together we were joined in a shared spirit, a spirit of hope, a spirit of love and a spirit of life. My autobiography was being lived alongside his. He had taught me that life was about living life. Before he could walk, he had acknowledged the anthems, and when I left him on that first morning at school, he knew what I meant when I said to him: 'You'll never walk alone.'

So I carried his dream to Istanbul. It was our team that would play out our hopes. And whatever the result of the match, I knew that he was teaching me that life has so much living, and despite the miles that separated us, we shared a greater power than any last minute goal. We shared passion not just for Liverpool FC but for each other.

As I drove away from home, he lifted his Liverpool shirt high above his head. He was sending me off with his blessing, carrying his dream to foreign lands. And more than this, he was giving my life reason. For he is my life, and I am the luckiest man alive.

Simon Jones

■

Green belt: help a child learn new and more helpful rules

One of the most powerful ways to help a child's self-esteem is to say more positive things than negative ones. It's easy to get caught up in criticism, correction and telling them what not to do. If all your young one hears about is what they do wrong, or are not doing, they may believe they can never do anything right. Give more emotion, energy and attention, as a conscious decision, to the good. If necessary, set up situations specifically to give yourself an excuse to praise your child.

We teach our children every day by what we say and what we do, and we are a big influence on the *rules* they learn. When your child does one thing right, that is a cause for celebration. As grown-ups we often feel we have to do *everything* 'right' before we have succeeded. Yet the child who is praised for playing a single, perfect note on the piano will be more likely to play the next one, and the next … and the child who is rewarded for a single act of kindness will be far more likely to do another, and so on.

These 'rules' apply to everything, and continue as we grow up
– including in our learning:

■

I arrived in Venice, and was met at the airport by a young
woman, no more than 25 years old. As we boarded the boat to
travel into one of my favourite cities in the world, she turned
to me and asked:
'Would you mind if we spoke English please?'
Not being fluent in Italian, I said an enthusiastic 'Yes'.
I asked her how many languages she spoke, to which she
replied:
'Not many. Five I think – German, French, English, Russian
and Spanish.
'And Italian?' I suggested.
'Yes, of course,' she said with a smile. I tried to think of
something to say, before she asked me the same question. I
was too late.
'And you?' she asked.
I quickly thought how short my answer would be if I also
missed out my native language, which I was tempted to do as
during this whole conversation she was speaking more 'correct'
English than I was!
I decided to include it: 'English and a little German'. And
then, of course, I did what so many English people do – I apologized.
She said: 'I think you speak more.'
It was not a question; it was not a tease (come on, David, I
bet you are really fluent in Finnish, Dutch and Portuguese, but
you are keeping that a secret). I didn't know what to say – I
didn't need to, she instead asked me a very strange question.
'Do you speak French?'
'No.'
'In French, the word for 'no' is 'non',' she said.
I thought: 'Brilliant, here I am in the middle of one of the
most beautiful cities in the world, and I am going to be given a
language lesson by someone just over half my age.'
I said, rather weakly: 'Yes, I knew that one.'
And she said five words that changed my whole approach
to languages, indeed, my whole rules of learning: she said:

'So, you can speak French.'

I didn't understand, so I said: 'Only a few words.'

Then she asked me: 'How many words do you need to know, before you say you can speak a language?'

I was about to say 'Enough to get by' when I realized the power in her rule of languages, as opposed to mine. Mine was, up to that moment: 'I can only speak a few languages. Besides, I was told at school I was hopeless at languages and that has been proved right. I only *speak* languages I am *fluent* in.' Her rule, which she shared with many schools in continental Europe, is simple, and it is this: the moment you know one word in any language, you can speak that language. All you have to do then, if you so choose, is to learn a few more words.

WOW.

Two rules, neither 'right' nor 'wrong'. I immediately adopted the second, and it serves me well – please, go out and help someone you know who is learning a language, or anything new, and give them the opportunity to share this new rule, if they so wish. I later discovered that we use very few of the words available to us, in our own language, anyway!

■

Black belt: connect with children, while helping them

OK, feeling brave?

When you read this next sentence your physiology may change so, in advance, take a few steady, constant breaths to put you in a ready state … OK …

If you would like to connect with children, pass on your experience and help large numbers. One of the most effective ways to do this is to speak at a school. Most schools in your area will welcome an external speaker such as yourself. It's usually easy to find a slot; the challenge comes when you actually speak because children are, in my opinion, by far the most open, honest and demanding of audiences. By far!

Please, do not let that statement concern you; let it excite you. And providing you do just one thing, you will go down well: leave the PowerPoint and photos of your last safari at home, and simply:

Be yourself.

Of course, plan and prepare. Involve them in activities and make it interactive – just whatever you do, be yourself. Tell stories, share experiences, and listen to them, and I promise you that you will enjoy it and, more importantly, so will they.

At a school in Greece, all of the lights, microphone and electrics blew ... twice. I somehow carried on – it was the best on-the-job training I have ever had! In Russia, a university student asked me: 'Of all your recipes, Mr Oliver, which is your favourite?' And in a British school, I decided to start my talk with a high-risk approach. It had worked for me once before ... I basically said to the children and teachers that everyone who had already spoken had said everything I was going to say, far more eloquently than I could ever say it, so there was no need for me to stay. The plan is that I then walk out of one door, along a corridor and then in through another door at the back of the hall, to continue with: ' ... although I would just like to say ... ' On this occasion, two doors looked very similar and I had not done my planning properly, so after the quote above, I said a very grand 'Goodbye' – and walked straight into a cupboard.

For your career

White belt 1: play Naked Coach Career Bingo

You may be familiar with Bingo. Usually played at a club, players have a grid with different numbers and the person running the game (the caller) selects numbers at random and calls them out. The first player to complete a line, or whatever the rules of that particular game, wins and shouts out 'Bingo' or 'House.'

This one is different, with Naked Coach Career Bingo I invite you to spot, or make, a contribution over one week, to win. What do you win? Well do it, and see how you feel. And see how your people react – and how your organization chooses to change.

Things to ask	Things to say one to one	Things to say one to many	Things to do
'What are your thoughts?'	'I'm sorry'	'Our future is our choice'	A presentation without a PowerPoint in sight
'What are we going to do to turn this project/ whatever into a success?'	'How do you feel about that?'	'I have a lot of time for …'	Welcome someone back to your company who had left
'How can we as a company help our community more?'	'I really love working with you because …'	'I know this has not gone well for us, and that's my fault'	Identify your successor and tell them
(In a meeting). 'Is that a true decision?'	Repeat back what someone has said to you	'I am totally dispensable'	Have a conversation with the receptionist/ cleaner
'How can I help you?'	'Tell me about yourself'	'Thank you' and mean it	Buy a small gift as a well done for someone in your team

White belt 2: bring yourself to work

You can picture the scene, because you know who they are. In work they are quiet, rarely contributing. Outside of work they are lively and sociable. It is like they have their personalities surgically removed each and every morning, and restored after work.

Have you ever noticed in life that, wherever you go, there you are? It took me a while to wake up to this, that I was and am the same person, the same mind, body and spirit, everywhere I go, and everywhere I am. Including at work.

We do not suddenly become different people at work, and yet so often it seems that way. Indeed, the collective conformity of an organization, along with structures, hierarchies and command and control, can squash people's natural personalities.

Since we spend such a high proportion of our time at work, why not enjoy it? Isn't it time for people to be themselves at work? You can do this each and every day, or just now and again …

The first international *Bring YourSELF to Work Day* was launched on Wednesday, 9 February 2005 by a team of business professionals, involving thousands of people working in large corporations, government departments, and smaller businesses, as well as the self-employed. As the campaign gains momentum, it is expected to reach participants in 120 countries and encourage people to have a fulfilling work life that is creative and inspirational as well as paying the essential bills. This is a not-for-profit day that anyone can take part in regardless of location.

Bring YourSELF to Work Day aims to create an annual working day when people choose to be more 'present' and more fully self-expressed in their work places. It is based on the conviction that too much energy is wasted by being one person at home and a completely different one at work. Once people have tried it for a day, the organizers hope it will become a daily habit.

On the day, people will choose to be more authentic by showing others more of who they are outside of their work lives. They may do this by sharing more of their dreams and aspirations with others at work, by being more relaxed and open, by talking about their talents and interests, by being more respectful or kind, by listening more, or by having some fun – any quality that comes naturally and which gets lost in the daily 'busyness' of work pressures.

The idea is simple, yet the effect of doing this will be to give others permission to be more self-expressed too, and a greater appreciation will grow of what we can bring to the job and to each other.

To find out more about the day, visit the website at www.bringyourselftowork.com

∎

Black belt for women: be successful by being yourself

I once wrote a column for a magazine, for women, called 'How to beat men at their own game'. It talked about the games that men play at work and how women can do it even better.

It provoked a huge response, mostly from people taking issue with my views. I expected such a response, and I expected it from men, who would feel cheated that our innermost secrets were being revealed. No, they were from women with successful careers, and entrepreneurs, who all made the same point:

'Why would be want to beat men at their own game, when we can be successful by being ourselves?'

'What about the glass ceiling?' I shouted.

'Where are all the female CEOs?' I replied.

'Women deserve more,' I whispered.

Then one day I was sitting in a fantastic presentation on leadership, and the top three skills for communications were raised: the ability to build and sustain relationships; the willingness to listen – really listen; and being prepared to show empathy and understanding. And so, at a risk of offending men, this time round, prepare for a very provocative statement:

The real skills we need to be successful in our careers, in our lives, in this world, are the skills that women excel at naturally, which we men have to learn and work hard at.

And overall these come down to the sadly called 'softer skills', which I would call the 'attitude skills', rather than those of aptitude.

Ironic that this quote comes from a contestant on BBC's *The Apprentice*, which managed to feature the most dominant, backstabbing women. It made great television, yet was not a true reflection of successful, really successful, career women today. Such as Julie Meyer, CEO of Ariadne Capital and founder of First Tuesday, www.ariadnecapital.com/, or Louise Makin, CEO of The British Technology Group www.btgplc.com, or Diane Thompson, CEO of Camelot www.camelotfoundation.org.uk.

I am not suggesting positive discrimination in favour of women, which is sexist in itself. I am suggesting truly choosing the best person for the job, and that women will be most successful when they are themselves.

Black belt for all: make yourself totally dispensable

There is one way to make yourself totally dispensable – by trying to do the complete opposite, by attempting to be completely *in*dispensable. It never works. As you gather and hold onto all of that information, protect your private network like a personal army, and play 'politics' at every opportunity, you are digging a hole for yourself that will not only cause you pain when you are pushed into it but, more worryingly, you will require scaffolding for you to climb out of it.

Traditional powerplays to make yourself critical to your organization do not work any more – everyone sees through them. The keys to future success are sharing, collaboration and the 'we' being far greater than the 'I'.

There are three main reasons why traditional methods of being indispensable do not work, for you, your organization, or for you achieving your aim:

■ Knowledge is no longer power. Relationships, leadership and teamwork are today's power. There is so much knowledge and information going around, and we have such ease of access to so much more, that holding onto your bit of unique information won't make any difference.

■ People who work to make themselves indispensable tend to cling on to their job role, and responsibility over others. Organizations of the 21st century, i.e. groups of people within those organizations, are waking up to the fact that their role, as individuals, is what counts, and to the fact that, since people will only ever do anything to the best of their ability because they want to, telling people to do something because you happen to be their boss doesn't work anymore, either. It certainly won't make you popular, anywhere.

■ The main reason it won't work for you is because your present organization is not your life anymore. Jobs for life are reducing in number and soon will be no more – so while your present organization may seem like your world, it isn't, and if you are made redundant believing that it is, that is what you will feel, redundant. You cannot be 'made redundant'; only your present job can be. You can do anything you choose.

■

A very good friend of mine was bored at work, and phoned me to ask the best way for him to be made redundant. It was a poor mobile line, and I was about to go into an Underground station, so I said simply: 'Speak your mind, say what you think, you'll be gone in days.' My entire journey I worried – was that too flippant? What if he actually does this? He will be out of work and unable to feed his family ... I called again as soon as I emerged overground, and clarified what I meant: 'Be professional, show respect for others; however, say what you think. Most organizations won't be able to cope with that. And be careful.'

And he did.

The first meeting he went to was on competencies. He suggested to the meeting that competencies is not the most powerful way to describe the natural talents and gifts of their most important asset, their people; and besides, it might just also be the single most boring word in the business lexicon.

After a long pause, someone else agreed with him, and then another.

He has been speaking his mind now for 18 months, and has had six separate promotions. He doesn't want his name mentioned as he is now on a fast track to be CEO of one of the most successful organizations in the world ...

▪

If you really want to be indispensable, there is just one thing that you need to know: *your skills, talent and gifts lie within you, not the role you happen to be doing at any one time.* Share knowledge and information, coach others to do what you do and, most importantly, identify, nurture and soon promote your next in line.

For strangers

White belt: connect while driving

▪

One day on the M25

There I was sitting in a queue, contemplating and cursing the traffic jam, when I suddenly realized, I AM the traffic-jam!

I caught the eye of a chap in a Saab on my left. It was one of those very quick, British glances, and we both looked quickly away. However, in that split second there was a connection: not between cars, but between two human beings. Two different lives, never having met, and probably never to meet again, being right next to each other at that moment in time, choosing to acknowledge each other, very briefly.

Then I looked to my right and saw a family of four – two boys in the back were waving at the drivers. I waved back and they cheered. I didn't notice the car they were in, because that barrier between us had come down. Then the cars, and people, moved on.

For a few moments on a hot day last week, in the middle of a tarmac motorway, I had the pleasure of making some very brief human connections that carried through glass and air and metal. And with those connections, my frustrations with the delay were instantly removed. It showed me that human beings can connect anytime, anywhere and anyhow.

Helen

■

Green belt: reconnect with a friend ...

When we lose contact with a friend, or a member of our family who has perhaps moved abroad, the excuses come easy:

'I'm not calling them, why should I, they never call me.'

'He's not interested in us anymore.'

'If she wants something, she knows where I am.'

And each day that time passes, thinking about doing something about it becomes more challenging, and the excuses become more overwhelming reasons, justifications for inaction.

If you want to reconnect with someone – whether it is simply to catch up, or if you do not reconnect with a lost loved one, you will regret it, really regret it – that is your choice. They may not want to; however, you would not be true to yourself if you did not make the first move.

Right now, at the back of your mind, who would you like to reconnect with? There are three ways to do this, all based on one principle:

■ *One: Easy – send an email.* Keep it very friendly, ask questions in the email, tell them that they should not feel obliged to get in contact with you, and leave your email address, your phone number and address. The key part in any email for the receiver is the third. This is always the one that automatically receives most attention and has greatest impact.

- *Two: Harder – make that phone call.* Again, the more general and friendly you make it, the better. Be prepared to do the talking – remember that they have not prepared for it, you have. And, as you speak, mentally throw friendship and warmth and love down the phone. Oh, and when you are talking, make sure you are standing up. By the way, this is also very powerful if you make a regular 'out of obligation' weekly call, say to your parents, almost as powerful as calling them out of the blue, at an unexpected time.

- *Three: Hardest, and with most impact, write a letter.* And I mean write a letter – if you send a card then write the letter on the card. In an age of immediate communications, the impact of receiving a letter is amazing. Don't type it; handwrite it. When you could choose text, mobile phone or email, if you take the time to hand-write a letter, that that says it all.

Black belt: give time to an older person

I believe we can tell the true values of a society by how they treat 'old' people. Sadly, too many now feel alone, of little value and scared to go out in public, especially at night.

Two things are certain, and one is probable. Certain: our population average is growing older and people are living longer. Probable: you will grow older (unless you die first). So, what are you personally going to do about it?

- Connect, really listen and show interest in, a senior member of your family. This person may well seem a stranger to you, outside Christmas, family gatherings, and of course their funeral, when you will have lost your chance. Do it without judgement, and show genuine care and warmth in what they are saying – they will have wonderful stories to tell and stories are there to be listened to. Never underestimate the impact that half an hour can have like this.

- Find a neighbour in your street who may need your help. Some people may feel too proud to ask for help, so seek them out.
- Join a campaign like Help The Aged (www.helptheaged.co.uk).

■

This one's for you, Mary

Rosalind and I went away for the weekend, and on Sunday we went to Salisbury Cathedral, and attended morning service. We were able to sit in the choir stalls – right at the heart of events.

I like to attend the occasional church service, and when I do, I simply absorb what is happening – the singing, the readings, the whole atmosphere. However, sitting next to me was a lady who insisted on looking after me! She pointed out how to follow the service, which hymn book to use and when to do what. She was so caring and kind I went along with all of her advice.

At the end of the service I thanked her, and learned her name was Mary and she was 78. She walked slowly with a stick, so Rosalind and I offered to help her home. As we walked she shared her family history, everything she knew about Salisbury, in fact talked non-stop, periodically apologizing for talking so much. She had nothing to apologize for; as we walked together arm-in-arm, I found myself truly living in, and enjoying each and every moment.

We walked slowly, and it took some 30 minutes to reach her home, in a small sheltered housing development. She said she usually did the walk in ten minutes, which means she either uses a skateboard normally, or it was me who was walking slower!

As we arrived at her door and said goodbye, something happened that I will remember for the rest of my life. She thanked us, and then burst into tears. We thought we had upset her in some way, but as Rosalind hugged her, Mary said she was crying with happiness because of the 'kindness' we had shown her.

And it made me think. Her route home was the way we would have walked anyway; walking with her was no inconvenience to us, and it was a privilege to listen to, and learn from her. I suddenly realized how many people of Mary's age, and younger/older, who feel lonely, and who value human interaction so much.

How many people are there in our families, our neighbours and our lives that we can reach out to in this way?

I learned a lot from you, Mary, in a world so bent on speed; you slowed me down for 30 minutes, and I thank you for it.

■

And a hidden black belt: help a homeless person

Hidden, because that is the way they seem. Hidden, because that is the way so many people wish them to be.

Sitting there on the railway steps, a youngster begging. We all reach immediate judgements:

- ■ 'Oh poor girl, I must help her'; or
- ■ 'Oh poor boy, it is so terrible' – and move on; or
- ■ 'Why don't they go out and find a job? – I haven't had it easy in life'; or
- ■ One of a thousand other emotions.

It really doesn't matter what I write here, and in many ways today's action is one of the bravest you will ever do. Because when we see someone begging we sub-consciously look around to see what others are doing – and as most people are walking past, that *tells* us that actually things are not that bad. And no matter how much I write here, you will either believe that, or you will not.

All I ask is this:

If you believe they really need your help, then next time you have a few minutes (that is all it takes), stop, give them some food (this will help any concern you may have that if you give them money they will buy drink or drugs).

Or

If you do not believe they really need your help, then next time you have a few minutes (that is all it takes), stop, give them some food (this will help any concern you may have that if you give them money they will buy drink or drugs).

Just one minute of your time. And just one minute of your empathy. We don't have to agree or disagree, understand or not understand, we only need to spend 60 seconds. That will be one of the most amazing minutes you ever spend, in your life, and in theirs.

Journey Five – Coaching the World

THE ANSWER'S YES … WHAT'S THE QUESTION?

The 100 plus most powerful 'How-To's in business coaching

Note: these are only powerful if you actually do them. If you do not, they will have no impact whatsoever.

Countdown (in impact order – sort of ...)

No.	How to ...	What to do
100	... identify the seniority in any meeting	The funniness of jokes is directly proportionate to the seniority of the person telling them
99	... win at Performance Reviews	Ensure your people have as much say as possible in sharing how they are doing, and ideally they 'mark' themselves – ensure they open up early in the one-to-one
		Remove the word 'average'
		When offering constructive comment, focus on the issues, not on the person
		Give specific praise – praise in context is very, very powerful
98	... speak with power by using the four most powerful words in the English language	Someone's name, 'because', 'would', 'and'
		Avoid 'try', 'should' and 'but'
97	... halve your time in meetings	Hold a 'what' meeting – a true brainstorm where you list the 'what's and then end the meeting

96	… create two extra hours a day – the ultimate in time management	1. Write down all the tasks you wish to do today. 2. Identify the five most important tasks, and number them in order of priority. 3. Start with No. 1, and do not leave it until you have either finished, or gone as far as you can go. 4. Only then allow yourself to start on the next item. 5. As extra items bounce toward you through the course of the day, deal with them only if they are of higher importance than the item you are working on. If not more important, add them to the list and keep working on your current task. 6. When the top five items have been completed, or taken as far as possible, or you have spent as long as you have planned on them, repeat the prioritizing process. At this point, include the other things you have added to the list during the course of the day. 7. Teach the system to your managers and use it daily.
95	… cause conflict in a meeting	Sit opposite the person chairing the meeting
94	… change your emotions	Ramp up positive emotions by using words like 'sensational', 'awesome' and 'fantastic', and reduce negative emotions through words like 'peeved', 'miffed' and 'mellowed'. Next time your partner upsets you say that you feel 'slightly grazed' – the emotion is less, immediately.
93	… put life in perspective	Go visit a hospice, and ask if you can be with someone who would otherwise die alone, or go to a graveyard and put flowers at the gravestone of someone you never met

(Continued)

No.	How to …	What to do
92	… WOW customers	Ensure people at the front line of your organization have freedom to make the decisions they need to make
91	… use XML output with SYMAPI commands	Ask your IT Director – if they know the answer … er … they shouldn't!
90	… feel great in the morning	Feel your pulse, listen to yourself breathing and hold your head high
89	… be energized beyond belief	Give out unconditional love to anyone and everyone you meet, including and especially yourself
88	… find a seat on a crowded train	Go as near to the front or back as you can
87	… know what to ask before your coaching session	If I knew I could not fail, what would I do? Who is in control of my life, right now? Am I feeling in balance, right now? Who are the most important influences on my life? What is important to me? What do I need to change/do, right now? Who am I, and why am I here?
86	… win serious brownie points in a meeting	Sit next to the most negative person in the meeting – when they go off on one, simply look down at your papers in absolute silence, with your hands clasped together. Sit completely still.

85   ... find peace now ...

Any thoughts you have that do not serve you – are not you.

They were not with you on the day that you were born – they are not a part of the true you. They have become attached to you, like Velcro, and they can become unattached, in any moment that you choose.

Perhaps, now, or perhaps, soon.

And the amazing thing is, you don't even have to believe me. All you have to do is feel whatever you feel, and think whatever you think – and it may be that any fears you had are slowly reducing.

That's right.

Whoever you are, and wherever you are, you may now feel a deep sense of calm. Of warmth, of love, of peace, flooding through you.

Very good.

And as you read these words, or as you simply go with the flow, perhaps you are now returning to your self.

To the real you, the safe you, the true you.

The you that always was, the you that always will be.

The you that is right now.

(Continued)

No.	How to …	What to do
84	… be a successful leader in the 21st century – these are the seven top skills	1. Self-Belief Knowing how amazing you are, and helping others to know the same about themselves. In any challenge, any situation, at any time. 2. Authenticity Be true to yourself – respecting the differences in others. 3. Personal Brand Everyone has a personal brand – a combination of reach and reputation. What is yours? 4. The ability to inspire – true leadership by being yourself Do you inspire people outside of work? Of course you do – by being youself 5. Global Vision For you and your organization, as well as for yourself and appreciating that you are the world. 6. Imagination and mind skills Working to develop an already razor-sharp mind and, recognizing the power of people's ideas and contributions. 7. Delivers Do you always deliver – and are seen to deliver? Aside from anything and everything else, do you ensure that you and your team actually does what you say you will, and carries through?
83	… prepare for a discussion on your salary with your boss	Ask yourself how much you are worth - not comparing yourself to anyone Be very clear in whose hands your income rests, identify that person, ask them what value you could bring Decide on a specific sum of money you want, write it down, and then … .

82	… get real	If you think that worrying about something will change it, then you are living on a different planet in a totally different solar system
81	… get the main point people are making in an email	If they write the words 'by the way', their key, most important point will follow
80	… turn around any crisis	Ask 'How does this event help us to achieve our aims?'
79	… respond to a very negative email	Don't
78	… destroy a blame culture	'It's my fault' – take the blame for everything
77	… get your people to love you	Take the blame for everything (see 78) and the praise for nothing. Always name another person for praise and praise the person – be specific
76	… see if you are a true leader – apply the acid test	If you were stripped of your title – the power to punish and reward your people – would you still get results out of them?

(Continued)

No.	How to …	What to do
75	… be a leader if you were previously one of the team	This is one of the most challenging areas of leadership, and one that requires specific attitude, behaviour and actions. You are now the manager, the leader, and it is you that will determine if this is going to work – not them. They will have their thoughts, their jealousies, and their whispers as to how and why you were chosen; it is up to you to overcome these through what you say, and more importantly, what you do. Follow this sequence of events and you will succeed: It is a given that the team has a clear vision and values. Identify anyone in the team who either applied for the role you now have, or considers themselves worthy of that role. Have a relaxed one-to-one with them and ask them how they are feeling. Ask them open questions and let them talk; listen and empathize. Never say that you did not want the position (why did you accept it then?) or imply that they deserved it more. Just listen and acknowledge any feelings, and close by thanking them for their openness and thoughts, and by saying that while some things are bound to change – socializing, etc. – you will still be a team, built on mutual respect and trust. Then thank them for their help in making sure this will be a success. Give them a standard that you expect of them for them to live up to. Do the same with the single most powerful opinion-former in the team, the person everyone refers to and looks up to because of their time of service or personality. Again, do not make it obvious you are singling them out – add this chat on to a normal work discussion, perhaps. If you have a team of under say 20, it is worth doing the above with everyone, in apparent random order and actually doing 1 and 2 first. Then hold an open forum, in which you tell them you will trust them 100%, while you seek to earn their trust as their leader. Share your style that you will adopt, and make sure you focus on projects and tasks to be done, as well. Do not say you are sorry to have the role; equally do not show superiority over them. If you feel really brave, invite the team to be the very best team of all time and then do a one-day transformation with the team (I know Naked Leaders and other coaches who can help you with this).

74	… speed up decision-making	Be yourself. Always focus on your vision as a team, on making true decisions, and on taking action. Be clear what everyone is doing and create an unstoppable unit. Do not be hard on yourself – you got this position because you deserved it.
		Model how you make decisions when there is a crisis and repeat this process when there is not
73	… get anyone to see your side of an argument in just seven words	'I am sorry (name) – you're completely right'– they will respond: 'No, no, I see your point as well.' It's called reciprocity
72	… improve your communication	Use lots of threes, e.g. 'hook, line and sinker' (check out speeches by George Bush Junior – sorry!
71	… impress in any meeting with just one contribution	At any stage say this: 'I think it is important to remember what we want to achieve here'
70	… find out what people realy want	Ask them!
69	… create winning teams	Put them together on the basis of their skills and strengths
68	… attract wow people	Recruit on the basis of personality
67	… deliver a successful project	Ensure everyone knows what is expected of them, have an open and honest relationship at the top of the project, trust the project team and avoid formal project management meetings …
66	… build rapport by email	Mirror people's style of email exactly when you reply

(Continued)

No.	How to …	What to do
65	… checklist for success	Ability to develop or adapt Inspires others Intelligent Takes risks Wide portfolio CV Builds strong relationships Outstanding listener
64	… checklist for derailment	Poor working relations Inability to lead a team Can't handle conflict Authoritarian Can't take pressure Few new skills All talk, no action
63	… get your child to go to bed on time	Say what you normally say, with the word 'would' inserted for other words you have been using
62	… commit to yourself	Write a letter to yourself and post it
61	… stay positive	Surround yourself with positive people
60	… secure the future of your company	Always recruit outstanding people and never feel threatened by them

59	… predict bad news in an email by its heading	It will be headed something like 'Just a quick email'
58	… be indispensable	Make yourself dispensable
57	… feel great	Listen to a piece of music you just love, and touch your thumb and first finger together – every time you touch your thumb and first finger you will feel the same. Perhaps you will choose the music you had at your wedding.
56	… feel lousy	Listen to a piece of music you just hate, and touch your thumb and little finger together – every time you touch your thumb and little finger you will feel the same. Perhaps you will choose the music you had at your wedding.
55	… find peace	Make peace with your father/mother
54	… go to sleep	Countdown from 300, in groups of 1 – 300, 299, 298, 297
53	… get on with your teenager	If you have a teenager, ensure their friends like you – that's cool. Also, do not tell them what to do (they will do the opposite). Listen to them and show interest, wait until they ask your advice, then give it
52	… bring success down to just one factor	The single difference between people who achieve success, and those who don't: people who always achieve 'success' give any and every event that happens to them the meaning that helps move them closer to their dream.
51	… be present	STOP – and focus only on where you are right now: the colours, the sounds, the moment

(Continued)

No.	How to ...	What to do
50	... create your own reality	Change the meaning you give to any event
49	... open champagne at a leaving do without embarrassing yourself by the cork flying into the ceiling	As you open it, turn the bottle, not the cork. Hold the cork still
48	... be charismatic	Be visible
47	... know the number one skill of outstanding presenters	Tell stories
46	... reduce the impact of a person	Make him/her smaller, silent, black and white and without movement. To increase impact, do the opposite
45	... trust your people 100%	It's up to you to earn their trust, based on who you are, what you do and what you say, in that order of impact, and make sure all are consistent. It's up to your team to lose your trust – and when they start to do so, tell them in private and show them how they can win it back

44	… know five key things about customers	Customers hate to be sold to, and they love to buy • Make it easy to buy • Put a person on the phone • Know them better than they know themselves – be prepared, look at their website • Be emotional • Be honest
43	… get a cynical person to smile	Get them talking about their children, or when they were once a child
42	… know that your worries and concerns are not you …	Any feelings or thoughts you have that do not serve you are not you – they have become attached to you, like Velcro. The incredible thing is, to experience this calm; you do not need to believe this. As you read this, and you are thinking whatever you are thinking, any negative thought or feeling you have is perhaps stripping away from you and even disappearing altogether fulfilling the promise of your first few seconds …
41	… be one team as you speak – the word to use in your team always	'We' – and when you use it, be clear who you mean
40	… when to benchmark	Never
39	… know that cynics are not born, they choose to be	Go to a maternity hospital and pick out all of the cynical babies
38	… be close to your children	Spend time with your children – when they want to spend time with you . It is gold-dust time, so do not be too busy or you will regret it when they grow up and leave home – and grow up they will. Watch their choice of programme on TV with them, and watch it positively without judgement

(Continued)

No.	How to ...	What to do
37	... impress a meeting chairperson	If they are right-handed, sit to their right, if they are left-handed, to their left
36	... present and be well received	Speak from your heart, ban the PowerPoint and know that everyone is asking themselves just one question: 'Does this person believe what they are saying?'
35	... give your children high self-esteem	Give your children high self-esteem by saying "yes" as often as possible, only one "no" when you want them to not do something
34	... how to handle the 'negs'	Put them in their place, right now. In 'public' ask them their opinion about something that you know they know something about ('negs' thrive on telling people that you ignore them).
33	... access the sub-conscious	Question to access the sub-conscious: after someone tells you they do not know the answer to your question: 'If you did know the answer, what would it be?"
32	... put in place a People Contract	*You promise to* • Guarantee their skill development (bonus – a skill unrelated to work) • Support them in this development • Involve them in real decision making • Open up real opportunities *And in return, your people promise to:* • Develop and apply the skills we need • Take collective responsibility • Behave in a way that is consistent with agreed values • Be team players with a commitment to each other

31	… be happy	Have a rule for happiness, such as 'I am always happy when I am above ground and breathing' or, as a team, 'We always respect each other as long as the sun is shining somewhere on this planet' – both real examples. The first person is always happy except when he travels on the underground; the second team always respect each other.
30	… control your self-talk	Control your self-talk – louder and faster = motivated; softer and slower = relax
29	… persuade	Know this – people are predictable. 95% of what most people think today, they also thought yesterday. Use this to identify what they want in life and frame your offer/idea to help them achieve it
28	… be happy (again)	Separate the emotion you feel in the thought by looking at it, as if you were observing it from the outside – say to yourself: 'How fascinating, I am having a negative thought.' Once again, it reduces. In a similar vein, remove emotions by observing the emotion itself, not judging whether that experience is 'right' or 'wrong'. So, next time you feel angry, say to yourself: 'Ah, this is anger.' The very act of observation gives you greater control.
27	… take control of failure	Give it any meaning you choose
26	… get someone to tell you their truth	Ask a question (one to one) – the first answer they give will be what they think you want to hear; be silent, their second answer will be the politically correct answer; be silent, their third answer will be their truth
25	… speak with an assertive/aggressive boss	Match his/her length of sentence and let silence happen

(Continued)

No.	How to …	What to do
24	… tell if someone is lying	Four most frequent signs – they touch their mouth slightly as they speak, they tell stories that are very elaborate and detailed, they may shake their head as they speak, they will not make eye contact with you
23	… give the greatest single compliment we can pay to another human being	Pay total and absolute attention – be with them, not with you. Meet their eyes. Listen.
22	… avoid 'copy-copy' syndrome	Reply only to the sender, do not copy everyone else – then the trail will end.
21	… be positive to children	Say 'Yes' as often as you can: *On the cliff railway at Lynton, about to reach the top. A mother took a photo and her daughter wanted to take the next one. However, by then we were getting off and there was no time. It would have been so easy for the mother to say 'No' or 'No time,' etc. Instead, this was the exchange:* *Daughter: 'Mummy, I want to take a photo.'* *Mummy: 'Yes, of course you can, darling. You can take the very next one as soon as we get off.'* *Daughter 'Thank you, Mummy.'*
20	… remove worry	Delay worry. Have a worry time in your diary – e.g. 3 p.m. every Monday or 7 p.m. every Sunday – when you will worry for five minutes straight. All worries and fears you have are to be reallocated to that time as you are too busy to worry right now. When that time comes, sit down and say to yourself: 'Worry', you won't.

19	… unleash ideas and imagination	Believe there are new ideas to be had
		Bring yourself to work and encourage others to do the same
		Recruit crazy people with crazy ideas
		Open up to other points of view than your own – read more than one book!
		Go talk to a school and ask them for ideas
		Hold a relaxation session
18	… help people's self-belief	Give permission, to everyone you feel may need it
17	… accept a compliment – genuine or otherwise	Say 'Thank you' and mean it
16	… identify a person's drivers	Ask a question and watch the way the person's eyes move. It will reveal their most dominant way of thinking, and whether they are remembering something, or making it up (constructing).
		Question 1 – 'What was the colour of the candles on your 12th birthday?'
		Their pupils move …
		Up and to the left (their left) – visual remembered
		To the side and to the left – auditory remembered
		Down and to the right – kinaesthetic feelings
		Question 2 – 'If you could wish for anything in the world, what would it be?'
		Their pupils move …
		Up and to the right (their right) – visual constructed
		To the side and to the right – auditory constructed
		Down and to the left – kinaesthetic internal dialogue
		Build faster rapport with visual people by using phrases such as 'I see what you mean' or 'I get the picture'; with auditory people say: 'Sounds great' or 'I hear what you are saying'; and with kinaesthetic people say: 'You'll simply love this' or 'How does that make you feel?'
		And of course, now you will know if anyone else is lying to you …

(Continued)

No.	How to ...	What to do
15	... change now!	Associate massive pain to any thought/feeling/behaviour you do not want, and massive pleasure to the thought/feeling/behaviour you do
14	... achieve instant calm	When someone says something negative to you, listen to the words without attaching any emotional meaning. In other words, listen without judging: simply notice
13	... live by Rule Number 13	It's OK to feel down, to be worried or fearful, as long as you are enjoying yourself
12	... build (even more) self-esteem in your child.	When he or she does something right, praise them personally – as one. When they do something wrong, talk about what they have done, not about their being 'naughty' – make a separation
11	... know the four things we all have in common	Friends, answers, influence and time
10	... have only one leadership provider	Ensure every leadership provider transfers skills across to people inside your organization – have only one leadership provider, yourselves.
9	... know the three magic words for all children from their parents	'I am so proud of you'
8	... transform communication in your organization	Change from push to pull, tell everyone where to go to find anything out which they can do without any fear or favour

7 … (women) – connect with your male partner — Ask them their dreams and how you can help them to achieve them

6 … (men) – connect with your female partner — Phone them, and make sure she ends the call

5 … get any voice mail or email returned — Leave something unfinished and hanging. People hate unfinished …

4 … WOW someone — Write a handwritten letter

3 … be one team — Be one team – agree with each other that you will never say anything behind each other's backs that you would not say to their faces, and put it into practice

2 … change Your Life – NOW — The fastest way to make any change in your life is to act *as if* that change has already been made

1 … quieten your inner voice — Say to yourself in total silence, and with love and belief, 'Thank you'

Journey Six

– Fulfilling the Promise of Your First Few Seconds ...

Journey Six –Fulfilling the Promise of Your First Few Seconds ...

HAZEL'S JOURNEY

Note: although Hazel's story relates to a specific department, the story, actions and experience can be applied to any. Indeed, Hazel's story can be yours …

1   The call

Hazel remembers the moment as if it was yesterday.

She was not only amazed by the timing of the call, she was also absolutely stunned by what he said.

It was her second year in Rome. It was originally only supposed to have been for three months, but she had loved it, and they had loved her. Head Office had reluctantly agreed to let her stay. Closer to the truth, the Italian CEO had not been prepared to let her go, until now, when he had to.

He never had the chance to warn her before the phone rang – a call that was to change her life, and many lives, forever.

It was Michael ('please don't ever call me Mike'), the IT Director. She remembers the exact words he used, and the thoughts she had as he said them: 'This call is confidential, Hazel. We need you to come back to London. We have some big problems in CS.'

'Never call it Customer Services,' Hazel thought to herself.

'The thing is, it's all going wrong, and we, like, need you to come over and help us sort it out. I have over 100 people, well, 165 to be exact, and they are all useless.'

'All of them?'

'If this doesn't work, I will have to outsource them all … but you'll be OK whatever happens. In fact, we will probably outsource them all in a year anyway – but we need to get something fixed now. So, whatever happens, you'll be safe.'

'"Safe" – now there's a word. And what about them?'

'Now, you are pretty good at motivating and leading and coaching and … well, can you come over and give it your best shot for a year? Then they will be gone, and you will be able to go anywhere you want …'

He went on like this for another three minutes, and the words got lost somewhere between his mouth and her heart. As he waffled on, her mind went into overdrive: *'Why on earth would she want to leave Italy, when she had worked so hard to learn the language, to master the culture, and to help make the changes that were needed? Was this to be the story of her life, some kind of dogsbody who travelled wherever she was needed? She had plenty of calls from other Italian companies. Why shouldn't she enjoy the benefits of her and her team's hard work? "No," she was about to say …'*

And then those two words echoed in her mind. *'All useless.'* She couldn't help smiling – the saddest smile she had ever felt. *'All useless.'*

Three thoughts came to her at once: *'I can't remember useless being on our competency measurement? I thought we said well below average …'*; *'What about Mike, sorry Michael, I mean? It was quite a feat to manage to recruit so many people of such a calibre …* ; and *'If they are all useless, how have they managed to deliver anything?'*

Then something inside her brought her back to the call. It was his final words that led to her true decision:

' … you will have complete freedom: you can get rid of whoever you want. We wouldn't call you but we don't know what else to do.'

She thanked him for the call, and for his flattering words, deciding not to quiz him about how this situation could have arisen, what was happening to the present manager, or quite why he sounded so desperate.

In that moment she made a true decision. She did not even pretend it was a logical one, or try to back it up with any evidence; she knew this was emotion shouting. It was time to say goodbye to Rome. After all, 165 people, 165 human beings – confused, unhappy and with apparently no potential whatsoever – needed her.

Over the next two weeks, she said her goodbyes, closed off the Italian chapter in her life, and checked her dictionary:

Useless
1   Unusable; not able to be used
2   Unsuccessful; unlikely to be worthwhile
3   Inept; not able to do something properly.

As her plane circled over Heathrow, a sense of excitement flooded her – she knew that the next few months were going to be the adventure of her lifetime.

2   The letter

Have you ever had the experience of looking at photographs from your early childhood, or when you were a student at school, or even just a few years ago, and wondered if that could have really been *you?*

That was how Hazel felt as she walked into her new office in the heart of the City, the financial heart of London. It was not quite her life flashing before her; more wondering just how everything she had done had reached this point, when she was embarking on a totally new period of her life.

Such feelings gave her a strange mix of fear and joy, as a new world of possibilities was just beyond reception, behind a revolving door.

As she waited, she watched. People were rushing everywhere and HQ came alive. She pretended to read their annual report (riveting stuff) while looking at each person – wondering if they were one of the hopeless ones. Suddenly Michael was standing in front of her:

'Hello Hazel,' he said. 'Am I glad to see you.'

Suddenly she wondered, all at once: *'Please don't tell me it's got any worse'* – *'Have they all resigned?'* – *'Am I on my own?'*

Michael continued. 'I came down myself, because this is all a bit *sensitive.*' By emphasizing the last word in a whisper it was the only word that could be heard by everyone around. 'I've booked a private room for us to have a chat,' he continued, oblivious to the number of ears that were now leaning in his general direction.

'When will I have a chance to meet the team?' Hazel asked.

'That might be a bit tricky at the moment. We haven't had a chance to tell them that you are coming over.'

'Haven't had a chance? Haven't had a chance! I've only managed to close down one area of my life, appoint my successor, sell my house, and say goodbye to over 200 people, and you haven't had the chance? What have you been doing? My God, if this is not your number one priority, what is?'

Michael led Hazel to a small, private room right in the middle of the IT Department. It would have been discreet if it didn't have such huge glass windows. As they walked together she noticed all of the looks that no one wanted her to see, closely followed by lowered conversations and fevered mobile phone calls. Yes, every single person in the category of no one knew exactly who she was. She could only imagine what 'exactly' meant, as she realized the spectacular own goal that was being scored right now.

By not telling anyone anything, everyone made up everything. Grapevines were growing fast, everywhere, and they all had one, common hatchet-man. She smiled as she noted the funny side of there not being the female equivalent.

'I think I should meet my team,' she suggested as they sat down.

'And you will, soon, and when you do, HR want you to read them this letter.'

Michael passed an official-looking letter on company headed paper, as Hazel noted the personal ownership he was taking when he said HR wanted her to read the letter. She read the carefully chosen words in front of her, and wondered how many drafts had led to this inspiring piece of legal jargon. She looked up, and was sure she could see a flash of helplessness in Michael. She passed the letter back to him:

'You said on the phone and in our subsequent discussions that I had complete freedom.'

'And so you do,' he replied.

'Well, I would like to do this my way, please, and …'

He interrupted her, 'After you have read that letter …'

She stopped herself – both from saying something that was bound to be heard through any glasses to the wall next door, and from imagining the beautiful fountain in the Piazza della Rotonda in Rome.

'OK,' she said, deciding to work it all out later. 'Right now, I want to meet my team.' And just as she thought that nothing else could surprise her, or that her company's non-communication could reach new depths, Michael calmly said:

'Good, they are making their way now to the main canteen, where you are going to speak to them in thirty minutes.'

'Thirty minutes,' Hazel thought, and then that inner sense of humour that voice that had kept her sane in so many insane moments in her life once again kicked in. *'Thirty minutes – you've never had that much free time in your recent life! What are you going to do to fill the time? I mean, you can't show your face, not yet. I know, why don't you go find that hatchet, and maybe do a streak through the office, see if they look the other way, then …'*

After reading the letter through many times, and being told that Gerry, author of said letter and HR Director (soon to be renamed Director of Talent), would be present at the meeting, Hazel and Michael joined the general rush of people heading in the same direction, towards a future they knew not what.

'Ah,' she thought as she was at last amongst them, *'here they are. Boy, have they got a shock coming to them …'*

3   The moment

The Restaurant, as it said on the canteen door, was already full to overflowing when Hazel and Michael entered. It was just as well there were so many knives laid out on the tables, as they would all be needed, given the size of the sudden silence that greeted them. Hazel smiled at people and was greeted with a mixture of looks – anger bordering on hatred, bewilderment bordering on resignation, and helplessness bordering on hope.

The silence was broken by whispers and then growing chatter. Most people were standing, many were sitting at tables (shades of

Oliver came into Hazel's mind at the empty spaces before them), and some were even sitting on the floor.

As they made their way to the front, she ran through the phone and email conversations of the last few weeks that had brought her to this moment. When she reached the front, a lectern and microphone awaited her, sitting on the makeshift stage the company cobbled together for all canteen addresses. And there, in the middle of the lectern, was a single A4 sheet of paper: yes, the letter was waiting patiently to be revealed.

As Hazel stood before the people she would now lead, in a manner of meeting them that was most certainly not of her own choosing, everyone went quiet and listened. She felt over 150 pairs of eyes tearing through her. She called on all of her experience, her energy, and spoke with a quiet confidence:

'Good morning.'

She received no reply, which did not surprise her. Resisting the temptation to say something like *'Oh come on, you can do better than that'*, she instead continued:

'My name is Hazel, and I am your new leader. Your former manager, Jonathan, has kindly agreed to stay on to ensure a smooth transition, before he leaves the company, and I thank him for that. Before I say any more I have been asked to read you a letter. Forgive me for doing this; I do not like to meet you all for the first time on such a formal and tense basis, however …' Her words seemed to run out as she picked up the letter. She read aloud:

'Dear Employee …'
She so wanted to add and say the three letters *sic*

'As you know the performance of Customer Services within Information Technology has been a cause of serious concern for many of your users.'

'Users.' She had asked to change that word, saying that there is only one other industry in the world that calls its customers users – the drugs industry. *'No wonder we are not loved,'* she thought.

'As a result, we are appointing Hazel Garnett as Customer Services Manager, and have asked Hazel to carry out a full and thorough competence review of the whole team,' – *'Yippee,'* she thought. *'So much more exciting than Alton Towers!'* – 'and asked her to report back …'

And she stopped speaking. When she looked back later, Hazel couldn't tell why she stopped at this point, or quite so suddenly. Perhaps hearing the words on top of her 30-minute study of them was too much. Maybe it was because of the inner smirk she swore she saw on the face of the new Director of Talent. Or it could have just been that at that very point all the last remaining hope in the room decided to simply get up and leave.

Whatever it was, she stopped talking, and what happened next would be remembered forever by everyone in that room. She looked up, a deep resolve in her eyes, and for the first time in her new team's presence, she spoke from her heart:

'Look, this letter is not me talking. It's not me. This is me,' she said, pointing to herself, as she came down from the raised platform, letter in hand, and walked forward to be amongst her people. She had lost her microphone, and found her self. 'This letter goes on to say that if my review concludes we have the wrong people, this department will be outsourced. Well, I have a Plan B for you all.'

At that, she tore up the letter. So simply, so low-key, so fast that everyone held their breath. Then she looked up again and walked forward until she was in the very centre of everyone. Most people could not see her, and started standing on chairs. She looked at them all, cutting out that inner voice that was whispering: *'That's it, you are now officially mad, and out of a job. This is not* The Dead Poets Society*, you know ...'*

She continued. 'My plan is that we create the best IT Service team this company has ever had. My plan says we do it together, and in my plan we do it in the next 12 months. We will create a team that we, our peers and our customers will be proud of. And then we will see, and measure, and ask how we are doing. And if we have not achieved what we set out to, and we are outsourced, then I will resign, because I will have failed you.'

And she stood in the middle of a canteen in a posh new building belonging to one of the leading financial services companies in the world, with a torn letter in her hand, and added simply: 'Together, let's build a true, authentic coaching organization.'

She did not expect applause, and she got none. Well, none in the hand-touches-hand sense, but the energy in the room had returned, and that was applause enough. She looked around. About a third of the people returned her look with support and huge smiles. Another third sort of looked at her, but not quite, as if they wanted to believe but they were not sure. And the final third looked away, as if they had just witnessed a public self-execution.

And then, making the huge assumption that she still had a job, she got to work.

4 Her first mistake(s)

As mistakes go, they were understandable.

Hazel decided the first thing she would do was to find out what was going wrong – after all, she had been called back to Head Office for a reason, and she knew that many things must be wrong if the company was about to read that letter out loud.

And she had to move fast – after all, the HR Director was now on the warpath, and the rest of her new peers, beyond the IT department, had at worst kept out of the way, and at best told her they were 'right behind her'. With a big knife, she thought, with less than a wry smile.

Hazel had read all of the management books – well, not all, but you know what I mean. Enough. Enough to know what had to be done. She had to find out what should be happening in this department, and what wasn't. And so she decided to find out by listening to her new team – every single one of them.

A bold move, considering there were over 150 of them. A brave move, considering most of them were not at all happy. A bad move, in hindsight, for four main reasons and many sub-reasons (isn't hindsight a wonderful thing – it's almost always invariably right, but it has one great failing: it's never around when you really need it).

Mistake one: Hazel did not have time to listen to everyone herself, so she chose her managers. They would receive her personal attention. Her noble intention? To ensure that all 165 people had a chance to have a say within two weeks of her joining.

Mistake two: Hazel brought in an outside consultancy to listen to everyone else, in strict rota timetable. Her thinking? To get an outside perspective.

Mistake three: everyone, Hazel included, had a set of questions to ask, all focused on finding out what was going wrong. A triple mistake, actually, this one. Her reasoning? Tackle the biggest problems and you get the fastest, most effective results.

Mistake four: Hazel and her new external consultancy team focused purely on the people inside her own new team. Her reason? She did not need to ask people outside the department as she already knew things were bad.

Now, as you read this you are probably thinking that those are all fair enough actions, taken for all of the right reasons. And that it is a bit negative of me to label them as 'mistakes'. We haven't got time for that debate right now. Because I don't want you to make the same mistakes that Hazel did. And neither does she.

Anyway, Hazel got busy getting busy, and in so doing she made the biggest mistake of them all. She jumped straight to the final part of the formula for guaranteed success – *Do it!* – without stopping to ask the questions *'do what?'* and *'why?'*

To be fair, Hazel was taking action; she was valuing the opinion of her new people; and she had put her neck so far above the political parapet that her head was now in the clouds, because:

- ■ *One*: Hazel did not have time to listen to everyone herself, so she chose her managers. They would receive her personal attention. This reinforced hierarchies, and sent out the message that the managers were more important than everyone else. These were the wrong people to give a clear, customer-focused view of what was wrong – from those in the front-line. And finally, this is the level that is most likely to blame other people: after all, as managers the present position was down to *someone* at this level – they just had to make sure it wasn't themselves.

  To be fair, Hazel did not have time to listen to everyone, and she did choose those people who would soon be her top team – well, some of them would be …

- ■ *Two:* Hazel brought in an outside consultancy to listen to everyone else, in strict rota timetable.

  Please don't get me or Hazel wrong. An outside perspective is of great value; but it usually comes with the agenda of finding something that needs to be done – by themselves. Foot-in-the-door thinking. Tell me, honestly, the chances of this consultancy reporting back to Hazel with their findings, telling her what she should do then saying a simple goodbye? No: the sound of problems is the sound of music to them. So, are they really going to say 'So long, farewell' or 'Can I stay and taste my first champagne?' Still, on a positive, an external view would certainly help …

- ■ *Three*: everyone, Hazel included, had a set of questions to ask, all focused on finding out what was going wrong. Oh dear. Focus on what is going wrong and what we must avoid going wrong in the future, and that is what we will do more of. Our minds automatically move in the direction of our most dominant thoughts – all day, every day. Also, wrong = blame (see One above). Finally, the very people who create a problem are not always the best people to describe it in an objective way. Nevertheless, they would be asked their opinion – something that had not really happened before Hazel's arrival.

- ■ *Four*: Hazel and her new external consultancy team were focused purely on the people inside her own new team (her reason? She did not need to ask people outside the department as she already knew things were bad). The biggest mistake by far – because Hazel did not focus on the people who really mattered: her internal business partners and her customers.

I'm sorry, David, you are not going to get away with that one – why would Hazel need to do this? After all, she had in her hands, on day one of her arrival … *The Internal Survey.*

Hazel's company prided itself on providing excellence in its internal departments providing service to the frontline, through them to its external customers, and on its quality. And to ensure that everyone was kept on their toes, as well as providing an indication of how it was going, they carried out a quarterly internal service survey (try saying that after a drink or two).The survey was an opportunity to praise each other, and provide constructive feedback on what could be improved, reinforcing that everyone was one team – all together as one. In reality the survey was to knock each other, and provide anonymous feedback on what was going wrong; reinforcing that internal politics was rife – all together as many. After all, it was a league table, and no one wanted to be bottom.

So, every quarter, people in Finance, Marketing, and HR, etc. were asked to comment on other departments. And they did. Including IT.

Because IT was such a large department, it was split into two: Systems Development (project delivery) and Customer Services (Hazel's area). IT Customer Services had been last in the league table for the previous four quarters in a row. And since they had only started the survey one year before, that meant they had always been bottom.

It was started as a business process re-engineering initiative, but that's not important right now. Besides, if I ever have to write, or think about those three words again, I might just jump out of the window. And I can't leave Hazel like that – even if I am on the ground floor.

No, Hazel had all the information she needed. And so she began …

5 Hazel finds the Holy Grail of customer service

One of the signs of great leadership is admitting when you have made a mistake. And this Hazel did, early on in her process. A second sign is to do something about it. She did this as well.

Yes, she listened to her management team but, early on, after the first few had answered her questions on what had gone wrong, she started to ask a different question. She asked: 'If you were me, the leader of this department, what one thing would you do, above everything else, to make our future different from our past?' And they told her.

Yes, she employed an outside team but, early on, she asked them to ensure that, for every piece of information they gathered, they provided a suggestion on what could be done about it; and, more crucially, she told them that any skills and behaviours that they had would be utilized – provided, and only provided, they were transferred to her own people. In other words, they must provide training, and teaching, and telling, and, overall, coaching, and from day one, they must work hard to make themselves dispensable. And they did.

Yes, she only focused on her internal team – until one day she was at the coffee machine. As you know, you can learn more from hanging around the coffee machine, about what is *really* going on in an organization, than in any meeting. And you can also learn who is doing what with whom.

Well, apparently. This is not always the same thing as reality. It is far more powerful than that.

So Hazel started to drink a lot of coffee, and this proved very good news for her career, if not her personal health. And the biggest thing she learned was so, so simple: she, and her new department, were not loved.

Now, she kind of knew this from the internal survey. But that survey did not talk about love, hate or other emotions that we, as human beings, experience all the time. No, the survey asked questions like: 'Is the service provided by IT satisfactory?' and 'Does it meet your expectations?'

Now, there is a very slight flaw in those wordings. They are meaningless, boring and irrelevant …

■

Do me a favour – persuade your partner to cook you a lovely meal. There is a very powerful 'how-to' to make that happen.

Simply walk into the kitchen with them and say: 'Cook me a meal, now.' Good luck with that one.

Now, the crucial bit is this: as you eat the meal, do not say a word. Not a word. Just eat. Your partner will be sitting there, wondering what you are thinking. Are you enjoying it? Don't worry – you will share this in a moment. Right now, you are eating.

And when you have finished, push the plate away, look at your partner in the eyes and simply say the following: 'Thank you – it was satisfactory.'

And then run.

And as you run, to appease the situation and win your partner over again, just shout out … 'No no. It met my expectations.'

■

… as Hazel learned next to the coffee machine.

But I will come to that shortly. Before that, Hazel did do something that would indeed move her off the foot of the internal league table – indeed, it would move her and her team up a full two places.

She noticed that two particular internal departments were not even included in the survey: Catering and Internal Audit. Hazel thought it was only fair – to provide an accurate, honest, meaningful assessment of how they were all providing service – to ensure that all departments were included. Hazel also thought that these two departments must rank as badly as hers. She was wrong – they ranked even worse.

So, for the first time since its inception, IT Customer Services moved up the league table, a grand two places up. And Hazel and her team rejoiced – but not for long.

After all, it was not the most positive of agendas. And there were no other departments left to include. And that is why one day, at a very low point in her life, Hazel decided to poison herself. She made her way to the coffee machine … the big one with all the numbers …

… and that is where she learned why words like 'expectations', 'satisfactory' and 'average' do not work. *Because, we, as human beings, do not think like that.* We never have, and we never will.

One day, in conversation with someone from the Claims department, Hazel pressed 1–2–3–4 (decaffeinated coffee, extra strong, white, extra sugar) and discovered the Holy Grail she had been looking for all along. That she and her team were not being judged by others on what they did, but on what people *thought* that they did.

Just by pressing 1–2–3–4 on a drinks machine and listening.

And in that moment, she suddenly realized … most people in her team did not wake up in the morning and say to themselves 'I'm going to go in and wreck the place.' So, performance, while it could always be improved, was nothing if people they were performing to did not enjoy the experience.

On a cold Wednesday morning in autumn, Hazel learned more about leadership, and human behaviour, and what to do about it, than she had learned from any book she had ever read. Thank everything for coffee machines, and the Claims department. And so she did something about it, something that would transform the team and department from bottom of any league table to winning awards.

Not yet, however. After all, she didn't know what she had to do, yet …

6 Hazel and the 'c' word

… but not before she had time to make just one more mistake. And this was a super one, a corker.

When Hazel had met with people and asked them what one thing needed to be improved, every single person said … wait for it … cue big font … massive … and capitals … and bold …

'COMMUNICATION'

Sorted! Improve, transform even, communication, and we are laughing. All the way to the funny farm. Hazel decided to take on board what everyone said, which was basically something like: 'We never know what is going on here. Please can you tell us what is going on? Tell us everything you can.' And so, she did.

She said to her top team, and to her consultants, something like: 'Keep everyone informed and up to date. Copy your emails and meeting minutes and anything else to everyone – unless it is confidential, personally or for the company, tell everyone, every day.' And so, they did.

And several things happened, all at once. People became enthralled as they read through all this stuff: it was so fascinating that little real work got done. Still, everyone knew what was going on. Well, they thought they did, until they cross-read the same 'facts' from different people, and discovered that not everyone was saying the same thing in the same way.

And then the excitement moved to intrigue to interest to passing glances to one day a girl coming up to Hazel and saying: 'Please, can you go back to treating me like a mushroom again?'

And so Hazel did – albeit a mushroom with intelligence. She switched all of her communications from 'push' to 'pull' – in other words, instead of she and her team and others pushing out data and knowledge and information that they thought other people would need to know, she ensured that everyone knew what they needed to do, or where they had to go, to find out anything they wanted to know, without any fear or favour.

And in so doing, people got back to work. And in so doing, the email systems became a lot lighter. And in so doing, Hazel made up for all of her mistakes, and more …

She also passed on responsibility to her overall team. It was now their individual responsibility to ask questions. Of course, Hazel still communicated with them – the headlines – but it was now their personal responsibility to find out more, if they chose to. And if they didn't, that was up to them.

In a masterstroke, she also removed the standard excuse syndrome that too many people thrive on. It works something like this: 'I know there is a meeting happening next week, but I haven't been invited. Just wait until they start the meeting and get to my item. I won't be there – and then they will be really stuffed.' All because of a simple error – a person not being invited. A simple mistake.

Now, it was that person's responsibility to find out what was going on. And, that was not the only thing Hazel did. She also mobilized her strongest troops, ready for battle, for she was going to win the war of perception, but there was another war to wage first …

7   Meet the Negs

During her first three months in her new department, Hazel spent much time in personal reflection. In simply stopping. She would go as far away from the office as she could, and she would just sit.

Not waiting.

Not with her mind somewhere else.

Just stopping – completely still. And it was in one of those moments that she made her next big breakthrough.

She thought back to the day she made her announcement. The day she put her career on a very thin tightrope. She was either going to succeed, big time, or … no, she decided not to go there. She remembered how she felt a split of energy in the room: how about a third of the people in the room had been so excited and inspired by what she had said. And at the other end of the scale, there were about a tenth of the people – perhaps slightly more – who had not looked happy at all. In fact they looked downright aggressive towards her – folded arms, heads down, like saying: 'Oh, here we go again. We've had other managers like you who think they know the answers, and they didn't, and neither will you. We saw them off and we will see you off as well.' The sort of people who don't realize the words 'self-destruct' contain the word 'self'. And then there was the majority: people who looked interested and confused, hopeful yet hopeless, excited but sceptical.

Hazel knew that each group was key in its own way.

She immediately decided to call the first group the Advocates: people who would always go with her and the team, who would always find a way, whose glasses were not so much half full as positively overflowing. She called the middle group the Confused. This was the group that needed to be convinced. Win over a good proportion of these people and she was more likely to be successful.

She struggled to think of a name for the last group. 'Losers' was a bit too much; and 'terrorists' was not politically correct in this day and age, so she decided on the Negs. Yes. And she also decided to do something about them. They would get three chances, and then they would be out. Hazel reasoned that most people in this category were simply wanting attention, and could be moved from this third group into the second. Besides, giving them attention, when their negativity had been thriving on never having any, was certain to confuse them! And that would move them 'up' one group. Three chances …

Chance one: Hazel walked up to one of the top Negs (what a personal brand to have) and sat down. She started a conversation with the people around, and after a few moments turned her attention to her target.

'Hello Neg,' she said.

Actually, she didn't say 'Neg', much as she would have liked to. She said 'Hello name' – actually she didn't … oh you know what I mean. And after a little chit-chat, which with Negs is often a lot more chit than it is chat, she said:

'I know you are working on the project to improve our customer reporting, and I wondered what your opinion is on how often we produce the reports.'

NAILED. She asked someone their opinion (everyone has an opinion) about something they knew about (the project they were working on) and – get this for the ace of trumps – *in front of witnesses*, the very people the Neg has been telling, forever, that Hazel and his/her other bosses never give him enough time or any attention.

Brilliant. Masterstroke. Actually, not quite – the Neg still has one card in their hand. They think it is the ace of spades – still, they may play it, but if they do, it is their second strike. Remember, one more and they are out.

Hazel has asked for their opinion, and this has delighted them. They have given it, and probably felt a huge sigh of relief, and value, especially in front of their colleagues and friends …

Or …

Hazel has asked for their opinion, and this has unsettled them. They have not given it – and probably felt a huge sigh of despair, and weakness, especially in front of their colleagues and friends. In this second situation, they reach inside their pocket and, in a grand flourish, they play their card. As they play it, they say something like:

'I'm sorry, I don't have an opinion.'

And you can almost see them smirk, deep inside. But it turns out not to be the ace of spades after all. It is in fact the two of clubs. Because Hazel simply says in reply:

'Oh, that's OK. Think about it and I will come back tomorrow.'

And when she does, if they do not have an opinion then, and if their other behaviour and attitude has been destructive, they have to go. And they did. Hazel was not prepared to risk the success of the whole team because of a few Negs. After all, if she and the team failed, they would be outsourced anyway, and she was not going to let that happen.

8   Hazel multitasks

Well, not just Hazel.

I think it is important, and critical, to say at this point of the story that I am only sharing the key developments, actions and progress. These fables are a bit like soaps on TV: we only see one story, indeed one thread or development in each story at a time, and we have to assume that all of the other characters and storylines are getting on with their lives at the same time, knowing that whenever something really important happens, the cameras will be there to pick it up. This is probably why we rarely see people going to the toilet in these programmes. We assume they will do that off camera.

And in this story, please assume, and know, that while Hazel is working very hard, the consultants have been listening to people, her top team have been working hard, the advocates have been getting on with keeping the department afloat, etc.

And that is a key point. Hazel knew the success of her department would not come down to her alone. Indeed, Hazel knew that she would play only a small part in the success that was to come. And that is why she applied the acid test of leadership.

She asked herself, every day: 'If I was stripped of all my powers – my job title, my given status, my traits of office, would I still get the best out of my people?' And with this in mind, and having learned from her earlier mistakes, Hazel did many things, the most powerful of which was:

She held Open Forums.

Or 'fora' as a Neg loved to tell people it should be, to be strictly Latin about it. She held them twice a week to start – Tuesday 8–9 a.m. and Thursday 4–5 p.m., to ensure not everyone was away from the department and to remove another possible excuse from the Negs ('Why does she only hold them in the morning – she knows I always work late').

And she always planted a tricky question – which she answered. And then the only rule was: ask and share anything you like, providing it doesn't go outside of this room.

When questions were asked, of Hazel or of each other, they were always given one of three responses. They were answered there and then, or they were confidential – in which case this was said, or if no one knew the answer, someone committed to finding out the answer.

She also did something around trust.

Hazel told her people – all of her people – that they had her trust, 100%, completely, and it was theirs to lose. She did not go into any fancy, long-winded ways in which they could lose her trust. Intelligent adults know what gains and loses trust. In return, she did not want them to trust her at all. She had to earn that – in their eyes.

So, yes, Hazel and her team did lots of things. But in terms of impact and results, they:

▪ Recruited on the basis of character, passion and personality;
▪ Replaced job descriptions with people descriptions;
▪ Replaced Service Level Agreements with Service Charters (free download at www.nakedleader.com/servicecharter).

And Hazel also asked that big question of all her people: '*Why do you work here?*'

No, that sounds a bit aggressive, I do not mean she rushed up to people and pounced on them and asked: 'You, why do YOU (still) work here?' No, in the course of normal, everyday conversation, especially over lunch (although Hazel was not very popular in the canteen after including Catering on the internal service league – and word had got around) and coffee and in casual conversations.

And she also stopped conversations about narcotics. After all, there is only one other industry in the world that has the term 'user' – the drugs industry.

Oh yes, and she and her team also did *the big three*.

9   The big three

One: Hazel plays politics

Hazel knew that to survive, personally and as a department, she needed to start playing politics (of the building relationships kind) as well as defending herself against others playing politics (of the stabbing in the back kind). And so she did.

She won over the trust and respect of her people (remember, the Negs have gone or are in the process of going). She did this by applying the stuff in this book (which is surprising, as it is still being written when she read it), and they all had one thing in common: she made it clear that when anything went wrong, it was her fault – even when it wasn't (she would always share a private one-to-one chat with anyone else involved if needed; otherwise accountability would mean nothing). And when something went well, it was never down to her. She always named another person who was involved and gave them specific in person praise.

She also made some very powerful friends. Well, three in particular: the Chief Executive (Clare), the Finance Director (George), and the cleaner (Christine).

She asked Clare if she would be her coach – and Clare said she would be delighted. Hazel always bounced ideas off Clare in advance of doing them, listened to guidance from Clare, and there was the added bonus that when any of Hazel's peers, say the HR Director, went to Clare to complain about something 'radical' that Hazel was doing, Clare would always say something like 'Oh, that's all right – I know what is going on.' Hazel was being coached by Clare, and Clare was being coached by Hazel.

She asked George if he would be her eyes and ears, to tell her what Customer Services (i.e. IT) was doing right and wrong. George had previously been someone who hated IT and everything about it; he was considered public enemy number one. Indeed, many of Hazel's people had come to her and said that she should not trust George, and should certainly not be his friend. To which Hazel always replied in a strange way, with just one word. Some people seemed to understand and get it immediately, while others had to go and ask what she meant. Whenever she was challenged or advised about George, she simply said: 'Tents'.

And that brings us to Hazel's greatest, most reliable fountain of knowledge, gossip and the grapevine. In these departments, Christine made Google look like a scrap of paper. Every night, straight after work, Christine would go about her business of cleaning – quietly, unassuming, in a world of her own, while the last few, dedicated staff stayed late, working hard.

Not.

Every night, straight after work, Christine would go about her business of cleaning – listening, assuming, in a world of other people, while the last few, dedicated staff stayed late, chatting away about what, why and, most importantly, who.

Now, to win Christine into her trust, Hazel had to do something very complex: the most powerful thing we can ever do to win anyone over, and it takes time. She treated Christine with total respect as a human being. And it took 30 minutes

Because Hazel knew that great leaders are always respectful and kind to, and value, people they do not need to be respectful and kind to, or value.

So Hazel defended herself against others that played politics against her – her peers inside IT. She did this through the above actions, by having a team who would follow her anywhere, because she did what she said she would do, and through delivery of both performance and perception.

And, talking of perception …

Two: Hazel has lunch with George

A quick word about Hazel's world – the world of IT.

Many years ago, people in IT support spent much of their time inside massive computer rooms. They had to be massive, because of the size of the computer, not to mention the massive cooler units – although I just did. And for security reasons these rooms could only be reached through a series of ultra-thick doors that made Fort Knox look like Legoland. And these doors could only be opened using a series of special cards that IT people wore around their necks. The scary thing is, they wore them on their necks when they were in the pub, as well. And probably when they went to bed.

Anyway, that cosy world all changed one day – and to IT people, it did indeed seem like just one day (it was probably a Friday). Up to that point, these people had been paid, and rewarded and promoted on the basis of their technical skills, on the number of words they could use in any 24-hour period that no one else could understand, and – of greatest importance – on their ability to keep as far away from other people as possible.

And then, one Friday afternoon, it all got spoiled. They were told: 'From Monday, all that is history. From Monday we must all become more customer-focused.'

Now, these were not clear or comfortable words for most people who heard them. Not clear – because they didn't even know that *customers* existed, so how on earth could they be *focused* on them, even if they knew how to do it?

However, they (and I am sure you have guessed, I) and Hazel, did not have anything to worry about – because on the Monday we discovered what being customer focused really meant. It meant whenever there was a problem, say when the system was down, simply putting on a pair of training shoes, and running around the whole organization, saying 'I'm sorry' to people, followed by quoting random times. I say 'random times' to mean the time given when the system would no longer be 'down,' but would be 'up' once again.

A key point on these times. They were totally made up (hence random) because nobody really had any clue whatsoever how long it would really take, least of all the people doing the running. Indeed, the reason we did the running was not out of urgency or to keep fit, it was because we had to reach everyone before the system was fixed, and that was the ultimate embarrassment – to tell people, as an expert in IT, that the system wasn't working, and by then it was. Mortifying.

Anyway, back to those quoted times … If you have ever been (or still are) on the receiving end of these, know this secret: the times quoted are directly proportionate to your perceived importance to the organization, in the eyes of the person quoting them. So, if someone rushes up to you and says: 'I'm sorry, the system's down, 15 minutes', then either you are a Director of the organization, you have just been promoted into a position of power, or at the very least you are very highly thought of. Well done. And, if someone rushes up to you and says: 'I'm sorry, the system's down, sometime next week', then either you used to be a Director of the organization, you have just been 'moved sideways', or you are the most lowly thought of person. Tough luck.

Soon, people were writing out 'I'm Sorry' on adhesive notes, and sticking them to their foreheads, to save time and voice-power. I even heard of one enterprising tattooist who set up a service in one IT department, tattooing the words on people's foreheads so they didn't have to persuade the stationery guard to give them a few adhesive notes!

And then, one day, for Hazel, all of this changed forever. She was having lunch with George (Finance Director) in the canteen. They were sitting in the corner, chatting. George could see the door; Hazel could not. Suddenly, having just taken a spoon of soup, George went blue, then yellow, purple and finally green. Hazel's first thought was 'I must avoid the soup,' and then she said:

'George, are you alright – what's wrong?'

George looked at her – directly into her eyes – then grabbed her arm, and whispered:

'He's coming this way. He's coming this way …' His voice tailed off in near despair.

Hazel looked around, to see a young lad from the help-desk walking towards them, quickly. Hazel remembered his name was Clive. Clive walked up to them both, politely apologized to George for the interruption, which for some reason seemed to cause George to freeze, then spoke very quietly into Hazel's left ear:

'The system's down.'

And then it happened. George stood up and shouted out loud, so loud that Hazel would remember it for many years, indeed for the rest of her life. Because what happened next was to change Hazel, her career, her team, her organization … her everything. What happened next was the second part of the coffee machine Holy Grail.

George shouted:

'He said it. He said those words – those words that don't mean anything.'

Clive walked – no, ran away, but not because he was scared of George. No, he was off on his run through the departments: and then George sat down and said the speech that, to Hazel, was more powerful than the Gettysburg Address.

'Do you know why I have that huge cupboard in my office, Hazel?' He didn't give Hazel time to guess an answer; he continued:

'To hide in.' Hazel would never have guessed that one. 'To hide in whenever I see anyone from IT coming along the corridor. I have to, Hazel, for my health, for my wellbeing, for my sanity. You see, you don't just apologize once; often, because you are so keen to spread the news, more than one person goes to the same area. Yes, you apologize in packs. It's like hunting – except we can't get away. And you don't seem to realize, do you …'

For some reason, he paused here, and took another sip of soup. Hazel was hanging on his every word, as by now were most of the people sitting close to their table. Hazel had the feeling what he said next was going to be kind of important. She was not disappointed:

' … that whenever we see you, it is when things are going wrong.'

And Hazel got it. She was not sure if it was professional or not, but she walked around the table, gave George a kiss on his right cheek, and simply whispered: 'Thank you.' And walked off. No, that's not quite true – she danced.

In that moment she realized what she had always known, at one level. Always known and never done anything about it. And then she started smiling – and on a random Tuesday lunchtime, in a canteen that was the second worst department in the company (Internal Audit, remember), Hazel found redemption.

She started singing to herself.

'That whenever we see you, it is when things are going wrong.
Therefore:
When things go wrong, we are going to see you.
Therefore:
You are wrong.'

And one month later, that had all changed. By using this same rule of human nature, in reverse, Hazel resolved to ensure that her internal colleagues, peers and external customers, caught her and her team doing things right, on a consistent basis.

She took a piece of A4 paper and a pen, smiling to herself as she, surrounded by a world of technology, drew a vertical line in the centre of the page. On the left-hand side, she listed the most powerful influencers in the company – with Personal Assistants at the top and those people who had been in the organization for years, even if they had never been promoted, also high on the list. She listed twelve people. And on the right-hand side she listed the most powerful communicators in her department – those people who could build rapport and trust with anyone, regardless of job title or length of service.

Then she matched the left-hand list with the right-hand list: on the basis of people who already knew and respected each other, on the basis of near physical vicinity and, hey, on the basis of gender, female matching male (by the way, if anyone thinks that is politically incorrect, remember Hazel did this, not me – take it up with her). And then, she shared the list in a private meeting with her twelve people, with the following clear-cut coaching advice:

'*Your job, in the course of your everyday work, is to ensure that the person you are marking catches you doing something right, on a consistent basis. Because if they catch you doing something right they catch us doing something right.*'

And so it was. And so it happened. In Hazel's world.

Suddenly, if someone on the list had a new computer, they would receive a visit to check everything was OK (after the IT person was sure that it was and any problems had been sorted). Suddenly, new friendships grew. And suddenly, Customer Services moved to the very top of the league table. And when they reached the top, Hazel had internal surveys stopped forever. After all, they were destructive, and others now agreed.

She still kept a copy of that last league table, though.

Hazel has one particular story she loves to share. Number one on her list was Clare (CEO)'s PA: Lizzie, a single woman of 21, who was matched with John, who was, so Hazel had heard from Christine, 'Maltesers for women.' Sheer coincidence, Hazel tells me.

One day, Hazel was getting ready for a board meeting. Before IT moved to number one, preparation for such meetings was very important, and involved Hazel dressing up in one of those American football outfits – ready for the monthly kick-in she always received from other board members. If it wasn't for her relationship with Clare, she didn't know what she would do.

Anyway, on this particular day, Hazel and the rest of the board were sitting in the boardroom, waiting patiently for Clare to arrive. While they were waiting, Hazel could almost hear her colleagues' fingers clicking as they warmed up for the monthly have-a-go-at-IT monthly gala. Indeed, on this day, things were not going well for the department …

After a few minutes, Clare came rushing in, sat at the end of the table and immediately looked at Hazel, smiled and spoke warmly:

'Before we begin can I just say what a great job Hazel is doing? Thank you, Hazel. I know you will all agree that IT is in very safe hands.' Hazel returned the smile, said: 'Thank you,' and looked across the table at George. Neither could understand what was going on.

This is what happened, that led to that moment, and to a major promotion for Hazel. Thirty minutes before the meeting, Lizzie, Clare's PA, had a small problem. Actually, to be more accurate, she was in a blind panic. The parent company's board meeting in Rome was due to start in ten minutes. She had an important Word document to fax over but she was unable to print it, because her printer was broken. And even if she could have, it wouldn't have mattered: the fax machine was also broken, so she couldn't have sent it in time, anyway.

That was when John walked past. He saw what was going on and asked if he could do anything to help. Lizzie did not mean to be rude, but, well, she was in a state:

'John, thank you but no, not today. I have to get this sorted and I now only have – oh no!' She looked at the clock in total fear '– twenty minutes.'

John did not give up. He asked what was wrong, and Lizzie explained. John then said: 'Look, Lizzie, if you would like, I can fax the document directly from the computer.' Which he did. It took him seven seconds.

Lizzie was stunned with gratitude. John left her, and then perception took over. One minute later, a nearby PA came over to find out what had happened. Lizzie told her:

'Do you know what John did? He faxed my document directly from Word – he reprogrammed it in front of my eyes! He is so clever.'

This other PA then repeated the story at the nearby coffee machine: 'Yes, IT can now reprogramme PCs, you know ...' And so the story grew and grew. In the next 15 minutes

And as Clare passed Lizzie, and asked if the fax had been sent, she heard the latest version, which was pretty much 'IT walks on water', which she translated as 'Hazel walks on water'. And after Hazel discovered the story, she went to John and said: 'Thank you.' – and I believe they are still, to this day, very, very close friends.

One final thought from Hazel on this 'marking'. I will use her exact words:

'Keep it secret. Senior people in your organization may say they want to be treated like everyone else, but trust me: they don't. Also, they would say they do not want special treatment. Trust me: they do. And they must.'

Three: over to Hazel

Thank you David, for sharing my story, I would just like to add the most powerful thing I did.

I applied my own formula for guaranteed success. Not yours, David. Our own.

And this is what I did:

1   Together with my team, in six minutes, we decided where we were going to go.
    - And we had no Plan B – it was a true destination;
    - And we had a very clear outcome;
    - And we did not over analyse it.

We were going to be the IT supplier of choice to our organization.

2   Together, with my team, we decided where we are right now.
    - We took ownership and accountability, and played to each other's strengths;
    - We decided never to say anything behind each other's backs that we would not say to each other's faces; and
    - We personalized everything – and if there was any stabbing to be done, it was to be in the stomach.

And we had a lot of fun together.

3   We knew what we had to do, to get to where we wanted to go.
    - We did much of what you have suggested, David, and also the complete opposite of much of what you suggested, and some new stuff;
    - We always made true decisions, fast; and
    - We acted *as if* we had already achieved our goal, our vision, or as you would say, David, our dream;

4   And we did it!

And every time we took an action, we simply asked if that action took us closer to our goal, or not. If it did, we did more of the same, if it did not, we did something else. We had only one *plan*, and many, many, many *ways* to achieve it.

And that is why we became, overnight, our company's
Supplier of Choice.
From

We are going to be the IT supplier of choice to our
organization

To

We are ~~going to be~~ the IT supplier of choice to our
organization

And we did it through coaching – coaches, coaches,
everywhere
And, as David seems to have gone off somewhere, I would
like to say this to you, just to you personally:
If you feel like doing it – do it.
And if you don't feel like doing it – do it anyway.
And realize now what it took me ages to realize:
Naked Coaching and Naked Leadership are not just about
David or me.
They are about us – all of us.

Now, please, go coach, go help others, go be you …
You will be guiding people to places that they didn't know
existed …
They will be excited, scared, motivated, challenged, curious
and anxious
All at once
You will make mistakes, you will learn, you will grow
I know you will serve them well
Please, please, go make it happen
Whatever your team, department or organization
Wherever you are in the world
And whenever you want to – as long as it is now.
Thank you.

INDEX